DISEASES & DISORDERS

Migraines

Anne K. Brown

LUCENT BOOKS
A part of Gale, Cengage Learning

GALE
CENGAGE Learning™

Detroit • New York • San Francisco • New Haven, Conn • Waterville, Maine • London

LIBRARY OF CONGRESS CATALOGING-IN-PUBLICATION DATA

Brown, Anne K., 1962-
   Migraines / by Anne K. Brown.
      p. cm. -- (Diseases & disorders)
   Includes bibliographical references and index.
   ISBN 978-1-4205-0219-0 (hardcover)
   1. Migraine--Juvenile literature. I. Title.
   RC392.B75 2010
   616.8'4912--dc22

                                                      2009050417

Lucent Books
27500 Drake Rd.
Farmington Hills, MI 48331

ISBN-13: 978-1-4205-0219-0
ISBN-10: 1-4205-0219-0

Printed in the United States of America
1 2 3 4 5 6 7 14 13 12 11 10

Printed by Bang Printing, Brainerd, MN, 1st Ptg., 06/2010

Table of Contents

"The Most Difficult Puzzles Ever Devised"

Charles Best, one of the pioneers in the search for a cure for diabetes, once explained what it is about medical research that intrigued him so. "It's not just the gratification of knowing one is helping people," he confided, "although that probably is a more heroic and selfless motivation. Those feelings may enter in, but truly, what I find best is the feeling of going toe to toe with nature, of trying to solve the most difficult puzzles ever devised. The answers are there somewhere, those keys that will solve the puzzle and make the patient well. But how will those keys be found?"

Since the dawn of civilization, nothing has so puzzled people—and often frightened them, as well—as the onset of illness in a body or mind that had seemed healthy before. A seizure, the inability of a heart to pump, the sudden deterioration of muscle tone in a small child—being unable to reverse such conditions or even to understand why they occur was unspeakably frustrating to healers. Even before there were names for such conditions, even before they were understood at all, each was a reminder of how complex the human body was, and how vulnerable.

While our grappling with understanding diseases has been frustrating at times, it has also provided some of humankind's most heroic accomplishments. Alexander Fleming's accidental discovery in 1928 of a mold that could be turned into penicillin has resulted in the saving of untold millions of lives. The isolation of the enzyme insulin has reversed what was once a death sentence for anyone with diabetes. There have been great strides in combating conditions for which there is not yet a cure, too. Medicines can help AIDS patients live longer, diagnostic tools such as mammography and ultrasounds can help doctors find tumors while they are treatable, and laser surgery techniques have made the most intricate, minute operations routine.

This "toe-to-toe" competition with diseases and disorders is even more remarkable when seen in a historical continuum. An astonishing amount of progress has been made in a very short time. Just two hundred years ago, the existence of germs as a cause of some diseases was unknown. In fact, it was less than 150 years ago that a British surgeon named Joseph Lister had difficulty persuading his fellow doctors that washing their hands before delivering a baby might increase the chances of a healthy delivery (especially if they had just attended to a diseased patient)!

Each book in Lucent's Diseases and Disorders series explores a disease or disorder and the knowledge that has been accumulated (or discarded) by doctors through the years. Each book also examines the tools used for pinpointing a diagnosis, as well as the various means that are used to treat or cure a disease. Finally, new ideas are presented—techniques or medicines that may be on the horizon.

Frustration and disappointment are still part of medicine, for not every disease or condition can be cured or prevented. But the limitations of knowledge are being pushed outward constantly; the "most difficult puzzles ever devised" are finding challengers every day.

A Nightmare Headache

I started getting migraines when I was about twenty-three years old. I remember the first one—I didn't know what was happening. I had a pretty normal headache, and I took acetaminophen and drank a lot of water. The headache didn't go away, so I tried drinking soda with caffeine, and my husband said I should eat something.

The headache only got worse. Lights and sounds started to bother me. The noise from the television made my head pound. Even a nightlight made my eyes sting. My head was pounding on the right side, like I could feel my pulse inside my head, and then I threw up. I figured I was getting the flu or something, so I took more acetaminophen and went to bed. I had a bad night—I couldn't get comfortable and my head hurt so bad. I held my pillow over my head and clamped my arm around it—the pressure was the only thing that kept my head from pounding and let me sleep.

In the morning, I didn't feel sick, but my head was still pounding. I threw up a few times. Lights and sounds were still really painful and made me feel sick. Any kind of noise made me want to scream. I called the doctor and made an appointment.

My husband was at work so I had to drive myself to the doctor. Driving was really rough. I felt like my pulse was slamming inside my head, and I couldn't see clearly—everything was blurry. The doctor checked me for symptoms of flu or a sinus infection, but he couldn't find anything. He asked a lot of questions about my headache and then told me it was probably a migraine. He gave me a prescription.

I went to the drugstore to get the medication, and as soon as I got home, I took it. I went back to bed and woke up about an hour later. I couldn't believe it, but the headache was completely gone. I picked up my kids at school and made dinner. I didn't feel sick or weak or anything.

I still get migraines about twice a month, and a lot of them are caused by stress. As soon as I know I'm getting a migraine, I take my medication, which is a triptan drug. It completely knocks out the headache for me. I feel lucky that it works so well, because I've heard that a lot of people with migraines

Approximately 30 million Americans a year suffer from migraines.

have a hard time finding medicine that works. I expect that I'll have to deal with migraines for a long time. They might never go away, but I sure hope they don't get worse.[1]

Approximately 30 million Americans get a migraine each year. Many migraines follow a pattern similar to the one that was just described. Some migraines are less severe, but many are as bad or worse. Severe migraines can send a patient to bed for two to three days at a time. Millions of people lose time from work or with their families due to migraine headaches. Many of those sufferers experience several migraines each year, and some have more than one per month.

These intense headaches have gained greater public discussion in the past decade or two. Migraines have become recognized and accepted as a real medical condition and not simply as an overreaction or drama on the part of a patient. As more people have come to understand their own migraines, they have openly revealed their personal experiences, sometimes as a means to help others. A number of celebrities suffer or have suffered from migraines, including Elvis Presley, Marcia Cross, Whoopi Goldberg, and Denver Broncos running back Terrell Davis, who was forced to miss the second quarter of Super Bowl XXXII due to a sudden migraine. Artist Vincent van Gogh, author Lewis Carroll, and scientist Charles Darwin were also victims of migraines. Migraines do not discriminate in their attacks and may affect anyone at any time.

Migraines are being studied intensively in the medical community. Researchers do not completely understand what happens in the brain during a migraine, and they have yet to find a way to permanently prevent them.

Nonetheless, new research and new medical technology offer hope to migraine sufferers. With advances in technology that let researchers analyze the brain, doctors are getting closer to understanding the process of a migraine. When the mechanism that starts a migraine is eventually discovered, people prone to migraines might look forward to a cure for their headaches or a method of prediction or prevention that could forever change their lives for the better.

CHAPTER ONE

A Headache or a Migraine?

Almost every person will suffer from at least one headache during his or her lifetime. Doctors estimate that at least 90 percent of men and 95 percent of women experience headaches. Headaches are the most common complaint heard by doctors from their patients.

Headaches vary widely in the severity of pain and the types of symptoms. A headache might be a brief "ice cream headache," commonly called a brain freeze, from eating cold foods. It might be a vague, dull pain across the top of the head. The most severe headaches can include blinding, explosive pain that is so excruciating that the patient can do nothing but go to bed until the headache passes, and that can take several days. More than likely, this kind of headache is a specific type known as a migraine.

Not all headaches are migraines. Some people substitute the word *migraine* for any type of headache. Some people think that a migraine is just a very severe headache. Doctors and researchers have come to understand that migraines have a set of very specific symptoms and often occur under specific circumstances. Anyone who has ever had a migraine can testify that a migraine is far different from an ordinary headache. Whereas a normal headache might feel like being hit in the head by a soccer ball, a migraine sufferer might feel like a meteorite has fallen from the sky and smashed him or her on the head.

Categorizing Headaches

Because headaches are so common and so different, doctors divide them into two distinct categories: secondary headaches and primary headaches. This helps them understand the cause of a headache and how to treat it.

Understanding the different types of headaches becomes a little easier by being able to distinguish between a *symptom* and a *disease*. A symptom is a physical ailment that appears because of an illness—sneezing, coughing, headache, and a stuffy nose are symptoms of a common cold. Bright red, itchy bumps are a symptom of chicken pox. A disease, on the other hand, is the root cause of an illness. Mumps, influenza, and measles are diseases that cause a variety of different symptoms in patients. Headaches can be symptoms, but they can also be a disease. This distinction is extremely important to a doctor's diagnosis, and it is the distinction that separates secondary headaches from primary headaches.

Secondary Headaches

Doctors describe a secondary headache as any headache that is the symptom of another disease. Secondary headaches are triggered by an illness or injury. Migraines do not fall into this group because they are not caused by diseases or other conditions.

Doctors sometimes use headaches to diagnose a disease. They must make certain to treat the disease, not just the headache. If a patient complains of recurring headaches, for example, a doctor would be unwise to continually suggest aspirin and bed rest. By asking questions about the headache and other symptoms, a doctor might determine that a patient has a condition as mild as a head cold or as serious as a brain tumor. For secondary headaches, treating the headache will not cure the disease, but treating the disease will almost certainly cure the headache.

Headache Assessment Questions

Doctors ask many questions in trying to diagnose a headache. Below is a list of common questions:

When was your first headache?

How long do the headaches last?

How often do the headaches occur?

What type of pain is felt?

Where is the pain felt?

What makes the headache better, and what makes it worse?

Do medications help?

Have you ever had a blow to the head?

What surgery or illnesses have you had?

How old were you when the headaches began?

What other symptoms accompany the headache?

What triggers the headaches?

Do any family members suffer from headaches?

Doctors need to diagnose whether the patient has a primary or secondary headache before proceeding with treatment.

Secondary headaches can accompany a wide range of ill-nesses. The symptoms of these diseases help to distinguish these headaches from migraines. Secondary headaches might be symptoms of the following diseases and injuries:

- rheumatoid arthritis, which causes swelling and pain in the joints, such as fingers, knees, and elbows;
- meningitis, an infection in the fluid that surrounds the brain, and is usually signaled by a severe headache and a high fever;
- a brain tumor or other brain abnormalities;
- bleeding inside the brain;
- a blow to the head, such as from a sports injury or acci-dent; or
- many other ailments, such as colds, influenza, allergies, and sinus infections.

In addition, people who are addicted to drugs, alcohol, or caffeine usually experience headaches when they try to quit using these substances.

Doctors can often determine the cause of secondary head-aches by understanding other symptoms or situations in the patient's life. By comparing these with the symptoms of a mi-graine, doctors can also quickly recognize that these types of headaches are not migraines.

Primary Headaches

The other category of headaches—primary headaches—includes migraines. Primary headaches are not related to other diseases or medical problems. A primary headache is recognized as the ailment that needs treatment. Rather than treating an underlying disease and thus curing a headache, doctors attempt to cure primary headaches by understanding and targeting the headache directly.

Primary headaches are unpleasant, but they cause no dam-age to the rest of the body. On the other hand, secondary head-aches might accompany an ailment or disease that could be

Tension-type headaches occur in people who are under stress. Researchers say 88 percent of women and 69 percent of men suffer from tension-type headaches.

fatal to the patient, such as a brain tumor, aneurysm, or stroke. The good news for a migraine sufferer is that migraines are not usually life threatening.

Doctors and researchers recognize four types of primary headaches: tension-type headaches, cluster headaches, migraines, and other headaches. All of these headaches are sometimes confused with migraines, but each type has unique elements that help to identify it.

Tension-type headaches are found in people who are under stress. Researchers believe that as many as 88 percent of women and 69 percent of men suffer from tension-type headaches. These headaches can be frequent—some people get several each month—or they might occur once or twice in a person's lifetime. These headaches usually cause dull pain in the forehead or along the sides and back of the head. The pain sometimes flows down the neck and shoulders. Such a headache might last a few hours or might continue for as long as a full week. One of the reasons why migraines and tension-type headaches are confused is the length of the headache; both can last for several days. Lack of sleep, poor nutrition, skipping meals, poor posture, lack of physical activity, and anxiety can all contribute to tension-type headaches.

The tension-type headache gets its name from the muscle tension that often accompanies this headache. Muscle tension in the face, jaw, neck, and shoulders is not the cause of a tension-type headache, as was once thought, but is another symptom of the underlying stress that can cause this headache. Migraines, on the other hand, rarely affect parts of the body other than the head.

Another type of primary headache is the cluster headache. Cluster headaches bring on a strong pain that feels like a drill is being pushed into one eye or one side of the head. The headache usually worsens for the first five to ten minutes and then lasts several hours. These headaches happen often—usually every day for a week, several weeks, or a month. This cluster pattern gives the headache its name. After a series of headaches, the pain might disappear for months or years before returning again. Most commonly, patients suffer from one or two clusters per year. Only about 1 percent of people are affected by cluster headaches. The cluster pattern helps distinguish these headaches from migraines, which rarely occur every day.

The category of "other headaches" covers primary headaches that do not fit into the descriptions for tension-type, cluster, or migraine headaches. This group includes headaches caused by coughing or sneezing or by physical exercise. It includes the thunderclap headache, which is an intense headache that lasts only a few moments. This category includes all headaches of unknown causes that are not related to other diseases. Some of these headaches are sometimes confused with migraines.

Migraine headaches have a unique set of symptoms. A migraine is a headache that lasts from four to seventy-two hours and is severe enough to prevent the patient from taking part in normal activities. A migraine gives a pounding sensation and usually causes pain on only one side of the head. A unique characteristic of migraines is sensitivity to light and sound—bright lights or noises might be painful, and a patient might seek out a quiet, dark room. Migraines are known to cause auras in some patients—strange flashes of light or other visual disturbances, such as blind spots. Another unique characteristic is nausea or vomiting—migraine pain can be so severe as to afflict some sufferers with intense stomach reactions. In the United States, approximately 10 percent of people are afflicted with migraines. Leslie Andrich, who suffers from migraines, shares her story:

> I remember that I felt like my head was going to explode—literally. It was so painful I thought I was going to die. I could never figure out what triggered one. The neurologist never gave me a diagnosis—just prescribed an antidepressant which really only deadened the migraine. Both my grandmother and mother have been migraine sufferers, and my headaches are similar.[3]

Looking Inside the Head

Because headaches affect different parts of the head and vary in severity, a reasonable assumption is that different headaches are caused by different structures inside the head. Researchers have concluded that this is true—the various primary headaches are triggered in different parts of the brain.

The brain is made up of three major parts: the cerebrum, the cerebellum, and the brain stem. Each part is responsible for controlling different aspects of human behavior. To understand migraines, two other parts of the brain are also important to know: the meninges and the thalamus.

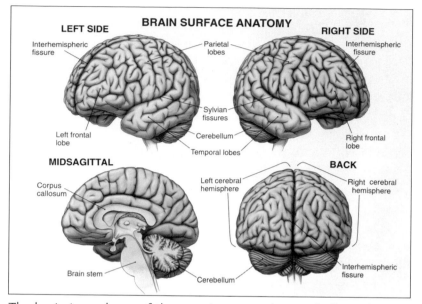

The brain is made up of three major parts: the cerebellum, the cerebrum, and the brain stem.

The cerebrum is the largest part of the brain, and it contains nerve centers associated with sensory and motor functions. When someone hears a bird chirping, tastes chocolate, writes a message, or kicks a ball, the cerebrum is at work.

The cerebrum is also responsible for higher mental functions, such as memory and reasoning. If someone memorizes a telephone number or solves a riddle, the cerebrum is doing its job.

The cerebellum is a smaller part of the brain at the back of the head, and it is home to nerve centers that regulate balance and coordinate voluntary movement. The cerebellum reacts to sensory information and is able to control muscles attached to the skeleton. This allows arms, legs, fingers, and toes to work together and produce coordinated movement. When someone pulls a hand away from a hot stove, the cerebellum is controlling the movement.

The brain stem is a bundle of nerve fibers and a combination of organs in the center of the head, near the place where the skull and the spine meet. It has a number of functions, including the regulation of heartbeat, breathing, and blood pressure. It is primarily known as the message relay center of the brain, and it delivers information from the body to the brain and sends commands from the brain to the body. When stimuli such as heat, cold, or pain are present, the sensations are sent along nerve fibers to the brain, passing through the brain stem on the way. The brain receives the message and understands that part of the body is too warm, too cold, or experiencing pain.

Sensory information—such as sights, sounds, and tastes—also passes through the brain stem. This allows the brain to interpret the incoming information. The brainstem also transfers orders from the brain to the body. When a person moves or speaks, the commands to do so are initiated in the brain and sent through the brainstem to the muscles.

The brain is fragile, so it is protected by a thick covering called the meninges. The meninges are made up of three layers: a thick, tough, outer covering; a thin, pliable bottom layer that contains many blood vessels; and netlike tissue filled with fluid that lies between the outer and bottom layers. The three layers of the meninges might be thought of like a sandwich, with a rubbery top slice of bread, and a soaking-wet sponge in between. The meninges help cushion the brain against impact to the head. This is the place where migraine pain is usually felt.

The thalamus is a brain structure that is important in understanding migraines. It is a small structure at the top of the brain stem. It receives all sensory impulses for sight, sound, touch, and taste, but it does not receive information for the sense of smell. The thalamus relays the incoming information to the appropriate parts of the cerebrum.

In order to function normally, human brains depend on a number of chemicals. These chemicals keep the brain healthy, assist in the transmission of messages, and maintain mood. Some chemicals function as a lubricant, like oil in a car, to help the brain operate as it should. One of the common brain chemicals is serotonin, which helps regulate pain messages traveling through the brain stem. Serotonin is a chemical messenger that transmits nerve signals between nerve cells and also causes blood vessels to narrow. Serotonin is believed to play a part in migraines.

What Happens During a Migraine?

Researchers know that they have not yet identified the causes and the progression of a migraine inside the head. Past theories proposed that blood vessels inside the head became constricted, causing warning signs, and that the blood vessels then dilated, causing the headache pain. Current theories indicate that this is only partly true.

In current research, doctors are considering about five different theories of how a migraine gets started. New theories regard migraines as too complex to be caused only by changes in blood vessels. A leading theory, called cortical spreading depression (CSD), proposes that the neurons, or brain cells, of migraine patients are easily excited. When a migraine is triggered, the neurons suddenly fire electrical pulses that ripple across the brain in a wave. The ripple travels down the brain stem, where pain centers are located. This ripple causes blood flow to increase sharply and then drop off quickly. The actual pain is caused by the changes in blood vessels, stimulation in the brain stem, or both. Headache pain does not occur in the cerebrum or cerebellum. This theory also helps explain visual auras such as blind spots and flashes of light, because the ripple stimulates vision centers in the brain.

Another theory about migraines suggests that the trigeminal nerve, a major nerve inside the head, sets off a series of events that lead to a migraine. The theory is that the trigeminal nerve fires and in turn stimulates arteries in the scalp and the meninges. It also activates nerve fibers that send pain impulses. The nearby blood vessels dilate, and inflammation is caused in the surrounding tissues, also causing pain. Brain chemicals involved in these processes may sensitize nearby nerve endings, which makes them more likely than usual to fire off pain messages. All of these pain messages then travel to the cerebrum, which tells the patient that he or she is getting a migraine.

Current migraine theory also suggests that brain chemicals play a role. Doctors believe that serotonin levels are unusually high before a migraine begins, causing constriction in blood vessels and a reduction in blood flow around the brain. This could account for migraine auras. Then serotonin drops to a level that is extremely low. When serotonin levels decrease, the blood vessels dilate and cause migraine pain.

Doctors admit that no single, definitive theory of migraines exists. They acknowledge that a migraine might be caused by a combination of the factors described above, and the exact mechanism of a migraine might be different in different patients. Further study will bring researchers closer to a true understanding of migraines and allow a greater chance of a cure for these headaches.

This illustration of one theory claims that a migraine is triggered by a malfunction in the synchronization of sensory input (arrows) which causes pain through stimulation of the trigeminal nerve (inset) and inflammation from leakage in the blood vessels of the dura mater.

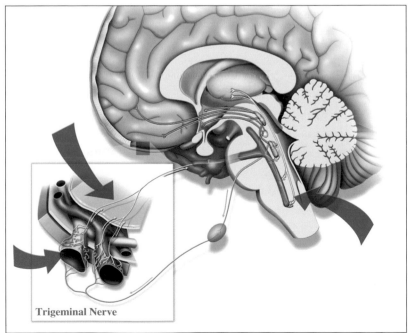

Trigeminal Nerve

Diagnosing a Migraine

Many people who suffer from headaches relieve their pain by using medicines such as aspirin, ibuprofen, or acetaminophen. These can be purchased without a doctor's prescription. When pain is so intense that these medicines have little effect or a patient's headaches are frequent, a diagnosis by a doctor is needed to determine the type of headache so proper treatment can be given.

Depending on a patient's symptoms, a doctor might quickly suspect that the patient suffers from migraines. However, some headaches, including migraines, are not easy to classify. In those cases, a doctor will also look for simple causes of headaches, such as influenza, colds, allergies, or dehydration. A doctor can quickly recognize symptoms of certain diseases, such as meningitis, and confirm or rule out such illnesses. If

Headache Danger Signs

A person should see a doctor or visit an emergency room as quickly as possible if any of the following situations occur. These can be signs of a life-threatening condition.

- A headache is sudden and extremely severe.
- A headache follows a blow to the head.
- Confusion or drowsiness occurs along with a headache.
- A headache comes with numbness, double or blurred vision, slurred speech, or the inability to speak.
- Lack of coordination accompanies a headache.
- The headache sufferer also experiences weakness on one side of the body.
- Severe vomiting or seizures take place with the headache.
- A headache comes with a high fever, neck pain, sore muscles or joints, jaw pain, or vision loss.

those ailments are not present, more information is needed to classify a patient's headache.

Doctors typically take a patient's medical history. They ask questions about a patient's past illnesses, accidents, or injuries. They also ask whether a patient's family members suffer from headaches; some headaches, especially migraines, tend to run in families. A doctor will want to hear a precise description of the patient's headaches, including the length of the headaches and the type of pain. Headaches can be described in many different ways—some of the descriptions include stabbing, pounding, throbbing, dull, sharp, aching, stinging, shooting, pressure, and pins and needles. Sometimes, the type of pain can help a doctor recognize the nature of the headache.

If the cause of a patient's headache is still uncertain, a doctor might order medical tests. These tests will help a doctor identify things that are not causing the pain and rule out secondary headaches. Some of the tests that might be used are listed here:

- A blood test, in which blood is drawn from the patient and examined in a laboratory, can rule out an infection.
- X-rays, like those used to examine broken bones, can identify defects or abnormalities of the skull, jaw, teeth, or neck. Unusual formations or alignment in the bones or teeth could cause pain.
- Magnetic resonance imaging (MRI) is a painless test that uses magnets to create an image of the inside of the body. MRI tests might reveal conditions such as a stroke, an aneurysm, a tumor, or brain abnormalities, and they can also examine the blood vessels in the brain to find anything unusual.
- A computerized tomography (CT) scan is another painless test that produces images of the inside of the body. It can detect problems such as infections, skull fractures, sinus diseases, bleeding in the brain, and tumors.
- A spinal tap might be used to detect an infection or bleeding in the brain. When a spinal tap is performed, a needle

is inserted between two vertebrae of the spine and some fluid is drawn out. Doctors can examine the fluid for anything unusual, such as blood or infection-fighting cells.

Not all of these tests are necessary for everyone who has a headache. Sometimes, headaches fit the pattern of a migraine so closely that doctors immediately recognize them as migraines without any tests. When tests are needed, doctors usually ask for one test at a time, examine the results, and then decide whether more tests are necessary.

If a doctor fails to find a sign of a disease after running all of these tests, then it is possible that the headaches are migraines. No single test currently exists to identify a migraine. When a diagnosis is made that a patient suffers from migraines, it is based on ruling out other causes and then matching the headaches to the typical symptoms and patterns of migraines.

What Does a Migraine Look Like?

Migraines can vary widely from one patient to another and even from one headache to another in the same patient. But all migraines meet a set of criteria established by the International Headache Society. According to its standards, a headache is a migraine if it shows a specific set of five characteristics:

1. The patient has had at least five similar headaches.
2. The headache lasts from four to seventy-two hours.
3. The patient has at least two of the following symptoms:
    A. a one-sided location
    B. a pulsing or throbbing sensation
    C. moderate to severe pain that prevents the patient from fully taking part in daily activities
    D. the headache gets worse during physical activity, such as climbing stairs or bending over.
4. The headache comes with one of the following conditions:
    A. nausea and/or vomiting
    B. lights and noises make the patient uncomfortable, and the patient seeks out a dark, quiet place.

5. A secondary headache is ruled out through a doctor's exam or a CT scan or MRI.

One of the first steps a doctor will take in diagnosing a headache is to compare a patient's symptoms with this list. If the symptoms match the list, the doctor will immediately know that the headache is a migraine. The doctor and the patient can then work together to understand the migraines and find ways to manage them.

A computerized tomography scan shows a patient's brain during a migraine. The lower left gray area shows the reduced blood flow and lowered brain activity that occurs during a migraine.

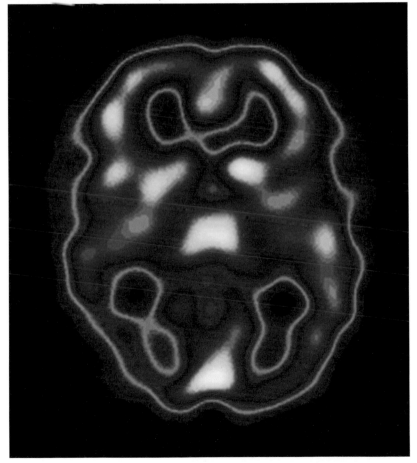

Ancient Headache Cures?

Fossil evidence from the Neolithic Age—around seven thousand years ago—reveals that in certain prehistoric groups, human skulls were sometimes drilled with holes. Anthropologists speculate that one of the reasons for this procedure, known as trepanation, was to relieve headaches. Many other explanations are possible as well, including to allow the entry or exit of spirits, cure infections or insanity, ease convulsions, or for religious reasons. Many skulls show signs of healing, which means that trepanation was performed on live subjects and that they survived the procedure. Scientists have no way to determine whether trepanation successfully cured any headaches.

A technician displays a surgical hole in a Bronze-Age skull that is clear evidence of trepanation, a prehistoric surgery that removed portions of bone from the skull.

Unusual Symptoms

Migraines can be difficult to diagnose. Symptoms vary among patients, and no single symptom is an obvious sign of a migraine the way pink bumps identify chicken pox. To make matters more complex, patients suffering from migraines sometimes report unique symptoms. David from Illinois experiences near-total amnesia during his migraines. As Miya Kressin, David's daughter, explains, "If my dad felt a migraine coming on, he would find someone and ask them to call his wife if he seemed confused, and he would give them her phone number. When a migraine hit, he wouldn't remember anything or recognize anyone except my mom. If you told him something during a migraine, he would have no memory of it later—except during the next migraine."[3]

Kressin also suffers from migraines with her own unique features. "My husband can sometimes tell when I'm getting a migraine. He says my personality changes. My handwriting changes, too—I write some of my letters in a completely different shape. It's like a different part of my brain is turned on."[4]

The wide range of migraine symptoms makes this disorder especially interesting and challenging to doctors and researchers. As painful and disabling as migraines are, their fascinating and unusual symptoms raise many questions about exactly what goes on in the human brain.

CHAPTER TWO

The Characteristics of Migraines

Migraines can make life extremely difficult for many sufferers. Yet a doctor's diagnosis can help a patient to understand symptoms and be able to predict the occurrence of a migraine. When patients understand the origin, triggers, and process of their headaches, they can better cope with this condition.

A Genetic Link

Doctors and patients have long suspected that a tendency for migraines can be passed from parent to child. Many migraine sufferers report that one or both parents also experienced migraines. Statistics show that 70 to 75 percent of migraine patients have at least one relative in the immediate family who also suffers from migraines. When patients understand their family history of migraines, this can help diagnose and manage their pain.

In 2008 the results of a study seeking a genetic link for migraines were published in Europe. Researchers worked with more than seventeen hundred international patients to find a genetic similarity among families. The project discovered a gene that is believed to carry the migraine tendency. Researchers Aarno Palotie and Verneri Anttila were excited. They announced, "This study is the first international collaboration as well as the largest linkage study in migraine [disease] to date. It successfully applied new analysis strategies . . . and paved the way for more large studies."[5] Researchers hope that more studies will eventually lead to a cure for migraines.

Doctors have long suspected that an inherited gene may be responsible for migraines.

Migraine Myths

Anyone who has ever had a true migraine can attest that the pain is very real. Yet many people who suffer from migraines are misunderstood. Some people think they are simply overly dramatic. Others may think that the person is just lazy and uses the migraine as an excuse to get out of work. Women with migraines are sometimes treated as attention-seeking. Some

Migraine sufferers are often misunderstood by family and friends, who may think they are faking the symptoms.

people have had the terrible experience of asking for migraine medication and being treated like a drug addict; medical personnel failed to understand that the person had a true migraine and instead thought he or she was just looking for a drug fix.

Because migraines occur with such a wide range of symptoms, they often go unrecognized, and a patient does not even realize that he or she suffers from migraines. A person's family and coworkers often do not understand what a migraine is about. Even doctors sometimes have difficulty diagnosing migraines. To make matters more difficult, no medical testing exists that can prove that a person has a migraine. This confusing set of circumstances can bring about anxiety for the person with the migraine and hard feelings among family, friends, and acquaintances. This is one of the side effects of migraine disease—victims often feel guilt for their condition or feel that they must explain themselves to others.

The Stages of a Migraine

Migraines often happen in specific stages. Doctors have identified four phases that make up a typical migraine: the premonitory phase, the aura phase, the headache phase, and the postheadache phase. Not all migraines follow this pattern, but headache sufferers and doctors can analyze a headache and compare it with these phases to help understand the headache.

Neurologist and professor Richard Lipton of the Albert Einstein College of Medicine at Yeshiva University believes that every patient must make an effort to understand his or her migraines. "Education and empowerment are the keys to successful migraine management. Patients who understand their disease, identify their triggers, and learn to use both behavioral strategies and medications effectively can dramatically reduce their burden of illness."[6]

The Premonitory Phase

Unlike other headaches, migraines often come with an early-warning system that alerts one that a full-blown episode is on the way. This is known as the premonitory phase—similar to

---

Tyramine

Tyramine is a natural compound in foods that is known to cause blood vessels to dilate. Researchers have no scientific proof, but they believe that the effects of tyramine can play a role in triggering migraines.

Many people who experience migraines see a concrete link between tyramine-containing foods and the onset of a migraine, and they avoid those foods as much as possible. Tyramine tends to appear in foods that are aged, such as certain cheeses, and liquids that are brewed, such as beer and soy sauce. Salami and sauerkraut are especially high in tyramine.

Tyramine can be present in nuts, olives, pepperoni, pickled foods, most beers and wines, foods that are dried or smoked, and mold-bearing cheeses such as blue cheese, stilton, and gorgonzola.

the word *premonition*, or a feeling that something is about to happen. It is also called the prodrome.

The premonitory phase can last for several hours or as long as two days. It often comes with a set of vague symptoms that are easily mistaken for something else. A patient may brush aside these symptoms and blame them on stress, lack of sleep, a virus, or overwork. A person who has had many migraines, however, might know what to expect during this phase and may correctly predict that a migraine is beginning. Premonitory symptoms include depression, fatigue, weakness, stiff neck, difficulty with concentration, frequent yawning, irritability, and muscle aches. The person may experience increased energy, a desire to work, or a craving for sweets.

Learning to recognize the symptoms of the premonitory phase is an important step in managing migraines. People who can anticipate a headache can then take medication, leave work early, or change their plans to help combat the oncoming headache. "A coworker of mine gets frequent migraines, and she's a master of working ahead," relates Deborah Weaver. "She's always several days ahead of her deadlines, just in case a migraine hits. That way, her work doesn't suffer and she doesn't have to play catch-up after she's feeling better."[7]

The Aura Phase

A significant clue to recognizing a migraine is a condition called an aura. Auras are disturbances in normal vision. They may occur as blind spots, sparkling white dots, or sparkling zigzag lines. They may also appear as a shimmer, much like a mirage on a hot road under the summer sun. Auras may cause

Auras sometimes start with a "flash of light" followed by blurry vision.

blurry vision or flashes of light. Sometimes the aura begins as a bright, shimmering speck that grows larger and larger. It develops into a blind spot rimmed by a shimmer in the shape of the letter C. The spot becomes larger until it expands beyond the field of vision. More rarely, patients report tunnel vision or "Swiss cheese" vision, in which their vision is restricted and they can see only small sections of what they are viewing.

Deborah Weaver has had numerous migraines, and her auras lead to temporary blindness, known as scotoma. Weaver explains:

> It starts with a flash of light, then I get a tiny blurry spot in the middle of my vision. Then I lose my vision around the outside edges, and the blindness narrows down until I can see only a small spot. I lose [that small spot of vision] and I can't see anything for twenty to forty minutes. I can't drive, read, or walk across a room. I can make out shapes and colors, so I'm not completely blind, but I can't focus on anything. After my vision comes back, my eyes are sore but I can function again.[8]

People who experience auras report that they generally begin twenty to sixty minutes before the start of the migraine, but they may appear as early as two days before a headache. The auras typically last about ten to twenty-five minutes, but they can last as long as sixty minutes. Auras are usually a clear sign that a headache is on its way; only rarely do auras appear without a headache. Researchers are not certain how many people who suffer from migraines also experience auras.

The ability to recognize auras is an important skill for a person who suffers from frequent migraines. When an aura begins, he or she can take steps to prepare for the oncoming migraine or perhaps prevent it completely.

The Headache Phase

The longest and most severe phase of a migraine is the headache phase. This stage can last from four to seventy-two hours.

In 60 percent of migraine headaches, the area of pain is limited to one side of the head.

The headache begins, often as a dull, steady ache, and builds in intensity over time. Sometimes, migraine sufferers can force themselves to go about their daily activities. Other times, the patient is in so much pain that he or she can only go to bed and wait for the migraine to end.

The headache might occur in a number of different forms. Most often, the pain is described as pounding or throbbing. In about 60 percent of attacks, the headache is limited to one side of the head. In about 40 percent of cases, headache pain is on both sides of the head. The pain is often concentrated on the forehead. The headache almost always becomes worse when the patient bends over or takes part in physical activity—even mild activity such as walking to the bathroom.

The headache phase also brings about other painful side effects. The majority of migraine sufferers experience sensitivity to light, known as photophobia. Any type of light other than dim, filtered light becomes painful, causing a stabbing sensation in the eyes. Phonophobia, an aversion to sounds, is also experienced during many migraines. Noises that are louder than even a whisper can cause the headache's pounding to worsen.

Nausea is another side effect of the headache phase. Almost 90 percent of migraine victims feel a churning stomach or lack of appetite. About 30 to 50 percent of people also experience vomiting.

The headache phase might also bring about discomfort around strong smells. Odors such as perfume, car exhaust, or certain foods might cause additional stomach upset in the migraine patient.

A variety of minor symptoms might accompany migraines; these symptoms vary widely from person to person. Although some people will not experience any such symptoms, others might endure several at once. These symptoms include sweating, chills, pale skin, diarrhea, bloating, constipation, a stiff neck, lack of concentration, anxiety, lightheadedness, and irritability. This wide range of symptoms can even differ from one headache to the next in the same person, and this fact sometimes adds to the difficulty in diagnosing a migraine.

The Postheadache Phase

Eventually, a migraine headache runs its course and comes to an end. The headache pain vanishes. Many people report that they sleep at the end of a migraine, whether for a short nap or several hours. Sometimes, the headache subsides after the patient vomits. Migraine sufferers might feel disoriented, depressed, or lightheaded after the headache ends. They some-times feel physically drained after their ordeal. In some cases, the person feels refreshed or energized. Regardless of the symptoms, victims of migraines are always relieved when the event comes to an end.

Migraine Triggers

One question is asked by almost every person suffering from migraines: What causes a migraine? Anyone who has ever had a migraine would like to know the cause and thus discover how to avoid another occurrence in the future.

Migraines in Children

Migraines might seem like an adult disorder, but they also af-fect a large number of children. Children under the age of five have been diagnosed with recurring migraines. One out of about twenty children (roughly 8 million in the United States) has ex-perienced a migraine. Up until the age of ten, boys and girls get migraines at about an equal rate. After puberty, however, the numbers of girls with migraines far surpasses the boys—girls get about three times as many migraines.

During the high school years, approximately 20 percent of students will get a migraine. These numbers decrease for boys in this age group but increase for girls. Some students report that they get two to three migraines per week.

Migraines in children tend to be shorter, lasting one to forty-eight hours. The pain tends to be all over the head rather than the one-sided pain that is common in adults. Drinking plenty of water and getting enough sleep are recommended to help children avoid migraines. Parents are also advised to monitor the consumption of trigger foods and watch for any related migraine episodes.

Researchers have identified more than a dozen different possible migraine triggers. These triggers are different among different people and can even vary from one headache to the next. Stress might bring on a migraine in someone at one point, but weather or motion sickness might start a migraine at a different time. This variety of triggers is another reason why understanding migraines is sometimes tricky.

Stress

One of the most common migraine triggers is stress. Stress can come from many sources—pressure at work or school, trouble in a marriage or other relationship, the death of a loved one, or the day-to-day pressure of always being on the go.

Researchers divide stress into two types. The first type is the stress of a life-changing event, such as a death, divorce, job change, or a move to a new locale. When these events cause a migraine, the migraine typically occurs as the event is nearing a conclusion—for example, after a funeral is over or a move has been completed. These migraines are sometimes called let-down migraines because they occur as a person is beginning to relax from extreme stress.

The second type of stress is the kind that comes with the daily pressure of work and family. After days or weeks of job demands, carpools, housecleaning, making meals, and other expectations, the built-up stress may trigger a migraine. In children or teens, the routine of school and homework plus the pressure of sports or other activities, a part-time job or babysitting, and household chores may contribute to triggering a migraine.

Sleep

Getting too much or too little sleep is known to trigger migraines in some people. These people find that staying on a regular schedule and getting about the same amount of sleep each night can reduce the chance of triggering a sleep-related migraine.

Noises and Bright Lights

In the same way that loud noises and bright lights can become painful during the headache phase of a migraine, some people report that lights or sounds can actually trigger a migraine. Loud music, traffic noise, machinery, car horns, or even the sounds of a large crowd at a shopping mall or stadium have been known to trigger migraines. Bright lights—such as streetlights or car lights at night, lightning, or camera flashes—can be migraine triggers. Sunlight, especially when reflected off snow, roads, or water, is another trigger. Sunglasses are effective at cutting glare and reducing the chance of a migraine. Some migraine sufferers take precautions by wearing sunglasses or ear plugs if they suspect they will encounter conditions that could trigger a headache.

Head and Neck Trauma

Head injuries often produce headache pain, and they can also trigger a migraine. A blow to the head—such as a sports injury or car crash—is capable of starting a migraine, sometimes within minutes of the accident. Neck trauma, including whiplash, which is caused by an abrupt stop or impact, is also sometimes a migraine trigger, even in people who have never had a migraine before.

Weather

More than three-quarters of migraine sufferers report that changes in weather can bring about a migraine. This may include the movement of a warm or cold front, thunderstorms, extremely high or low humidity, or an abrupt drop in atmospheric pressure.

Robyn Sanicki knows that weather is responsible for most of her migraines. "My migraines get started when the pressure fronts come through. It's like I have a barometer inside my head, and certain changes get a migraine going. The good thing is that weather sometimes warns me that a migraine is getting ready to happen."[9]

Odor Triggers

Just as some people can become highly sensitive to strong smells during the headache phase of a migraine, certain odors are also known to trigger migraines. These are smells such as car exhaust, tobacco smoke, perfumes and aftershaves, paint, and chemicals. The effect of these smells is worse in a confined space, such as an airplane or elevator. Nancy Milde-brandt, who suffers from migraines, relates:

> Years ago, I worked in an office building that had a fast food restaurant. Sometimes the smell would leak into our office. I was getting a migraine and could smell the food, and I told my boss I had to go home. I really thought I was going to throw up.

Many migraine sufferers cannot walk by perfume displays because the smell of perfume can trigger a migraine attack.

I also can't walk though the perfume department at a department store. There's a really good chance that the smell will give me a migraine.[10]

Motion Sickness

Research shows that migraine sufferers are more prone to motion sickness than are people who do not get migraines. Evidence also suggests that adults who experience migraines likely suffered from motion sickness in childhood. The connection between motion sickness and migraines is not understood. Motion sickness also appears to be a migraine trigger for some people.

Hormones

Hormones are natural chemicals produced by the body to regulate a variety of functions, including growth, puberty, pregnancy, and menopause. Changes in hormone levels are known to cause migraines. Women go through a cycle of hormones every month, and their hormones change dramatically during pregnancy. Many women report that their migraines are brought on at certain times of the month or during or after pregnancy. Marilyn Hartman knows that her migraines were linked to hormones because they improved after she went through menopause and her hormone activity decreased. "I got my first migraine when I was thirty-five years old. After that, I had a headache every day for sixteen years, with a migraine once or twice a week. After I reached menopause, the migraines mostly went away. I'm still sensitive to bright light and glare, especially bright sun on the snow in winter."[11]

Miscellaneous Triggers

The list of migraine triggers is long. Some triggers are very common, but certain others are rare or unusual. Some less common triggers are fluorescent lighting, certain prescription medications, strenuous exercise, dehydration, smoking, secondhand smoke, and combined environmental factors such as air conditioning, office or industrial machinery, and plastic or vinyl smells. For some people, these individual triggers do not cause migraines, but specific combinations will set off the headache. For example, air conditioning might not start a headache, but the combination of air conditioning, fluorescent lighting, and machinery noises might bring on a migraine.

Foods

Some of the best-known and most common migraine triggers are foods. These triggers tend to vary by person; whereas some people have no food triggers, others are highly sensitive to many foods.

People prone to migraines are often instructed to pay attention to their diet in order to avoid trigger foods. This means that a food like pizza needs to be eaten with care; pizza may

For some people prone to migraines, eating pizza can trigger an attack. Others may suffer no ill effects from the food.

Migraines and Food

Although no statistics reveal exactly how many migraine sufferers have specific food triggers related to their migraines, some commonality exists. Common food triggers are those foods that most migraine sufferers must avoid. But other less common, and even unusual, food triggers also exist for some migraine sufferers.

Common Food Triggers
- Aged cheeses, such as sharp cheddar or blue cheese
- Alcoholic beverages
- Aspartame (an artificial sweetener found in diet soda and other foods)
- Caffeine
- Chocolate
- MSG (monosodium glutamate, a food preservative and flavor enhancer)
- Red wine
- Sulfites (preservatives often used in dried fruits or wine)
- Sodium nitrate and sodium nitrite (food preservatives found in hot dogs, lunch meat, and sausage)

Uncommon Food Triggers
- Avocados
- Bananas
- Citrus fruits and juices
- Dairy products, such as sour cream, buttermilk, and yogurt
- Garlic
- Onions
- Pickled foods, such as herring, sauerkraut, and pickles
- Yeast, baker's

Unusual Food Triggers
- Figs
- Legumes (beans, peas, peanuts, soybeans)
- Nuts (any kind)
- Olives
- Papaya
- Pineapple
- Tomatoes

contain tomatoes, onions, garlic, sausage, and cheese—all of which are on the trigger list. For a person who experiences none of these triggers, pizza may be perfectly safe; for others, however, it may be a one-way ticket to bed rest in order to cope with a migraine.

In the category of food triggers, caffeine and chocolate deserve special mention. Whereas some people report that these are migraine triggers, others crave these foods during migraines. Still others claim that caffeine or chocolate actually help to calm down the headache. Caffeine is a common ingredient in some over-the-counter headache and migraine pain relievers. People prone to migraines are wise to pay attention to the effects of these substances and add or subtract them from their diets to better manage their migraines.

More unusual, some foods become triggers only when in combination with other foods. Nancy Mildebrandt has to avoid chocolate and cheese on the same day. "I can eat chocolate without problems, and I can eat cheese. But if I eat one of them, and then eat the other on the same day, I'm almost certain to get a migraine."[12]

For those suffering from migraines, discovering triggers is like striking gold. Each time they identify a new trigger, they have a greater ability to manage their migraines. By avoiding these triggers, they can greatly reduce the number of headaches that occur or be prepared for headaches once they start. Every migraine is a learning process; people who experience migraines continually analyze their lives and their headaches to discover ways to reduce the impact of migraines.

CHAPTER THREE

The Migraine Lifestyle

Most people get up in the morning and face a busy schedule or a long list of tasks that need to be accomplished. They probably go to work or school, and they might have to care for a family. They might be on sports teams or have an exercise routine, and they might have hobbies or activities to attend. For someone who gets frequent migraines, every day begins with a question: Will this be a migraine day?

Some migraines force a person to stay in bed, but others might allow him or her to struggle through the day. Either way, the headaches can disrupt or ruin a person's day. This is true for the nearly 30 million people who suffer from migraines each year in the United States. The World Health Organization estimates that 303 million people worldwide are afflicted with migraines. Migraines can affect children as young as age two, but they are most common in people aged twenty-five to forty-five. Migraine episodes are more common in women than in men, affecting 12 to 18 percent of women and 6 to 8 percent of men. In total, 16 to 17 percent of people will get a migraine during their lifetime. Thus, a great number of people are trying to cope with a migraine on any given day.

Migraines are difficult to live with and complex to understand. Yet when people analyze their migraines and make an effort to understand them, they take a huge step toward minimizing the amount of time that they suffer. Doctors and patients have discovered a number of ways to recognize, identify, and shorten migraine episodes.

Managing Triggers

The causes of migraines are not understood, and those causes vary a great deal from person to person. Over time, most migraine sufferers learn to recognize at least some of their triggers. Approximately 85 percent of people with migraines can identify at least one trigger.

Some triggers cannot be avoided, such as hormones, changes in the weather, or the noises and smells associated with traffic. People who have these triggers might carry medication with them, however, so they can begin treatment if they suspect the beginning of a migraine.

Other triggers, such as food, smoking, lack of sleep, or loud music can be easier to manage. Avoiding these triggers might be inconvenient at times—skipping a pizza or turning down music might not seem like much fun—but the alternative of a full-blown migraine is far worse. Doctors recommend that migraine patients make an effort to understand and avoid their triggers.

People prone to migraines must manage their triggers, which may include loud music.

Detecting the Warning Signs

Even when a person makes every effort to control his or her lifestyle, migraines can still take hold. Many people report good success in avoiding a migraine if they take steps as soon as they recognize a warning signal. This might mean taking medication, grabbing a quick nap, or finding a dark, quiet place for a break.

During Super Bowl XXXII in 1998, Denver Broncos running back Terrell Davis recognized his oncoming migraine. "In all the games I've ever played in my life, it had to come on this Sunday. I noticed I had a headache . . . I couldn't see." He left the game to take his medication, missed the second quarter, and returned to the game after halftime. "I remember late in the game thinking . . . man . . . I don't want to lose—not now. I don't want to lose right now."[13] Davis's medication succeeded in blocking the migraine. He scored three touchdowns in the game and was voted Most Valuable Player. The Denver Broncos defeated the Green Bay Packers to win the Super Bowl.

Not all migraines are blocked with this level of success, but early intervention can make all the difference in avoiding an episode. Many migraine sufferers report that taking medication at the first warning sign is the key to getting relief.

Keeping a Migraine Journal

Experienced migraine sufferers generally have some clues about how and when their migraines get started. They might know what foods, factors, or weather are likely to start a migraine. They might also know that lack of sleep or the noise of a shopping mall could bring on a migraine and take steps to get enough rest or visit the mall during quieter hours. Multiple migraines provide important information as to triggers or warning signs.

Most doctors recommend that migraine patients keep a journal. In the journal, they record all of the foods they eat, their activities, and any unusual symptoms they may feel. Any symptom, no matter how minor, can be important. Feelings of tiredness, depression, weakness, or dizziness can all be pre-

Doctors recommend that migraine patients keep a journal, recording what they eat, the activities they participate in, and any unusual symptoms they may feel.

monitory symptoms, although many people may brush them off as insignificant.

When a migraine occurs, patients record all of the symptoms and any medications they take. They also record any factors that make the headache better or worse. Then, when a migraine is over, a patient can look back at the journal and try to detect any triggers or warning signs. After several migraines, patients might discover a pattern—for example, that they ate a certain food, got stuck in traffic on a hot day, or experienced a high level of stress. Because changes in weather can be a factor in migraines, weather conditions are also recorded in the journal.

Wayne Hoffmann discovered patterns in his migraines. "I didn't get migraines very often," he says, "but when I did, they put me in bed for two days. I figured out that they hit me after major stressful events. Then I read an article about food triggers and realized that red wine and blue cheese would cause headaches for me. It was easy to avoid those foods after that, and it cut down on the number of migraines I would get."[14]

Headache Maps

Another effective way to evaluate and record headaches is to draw a map or picture. Describing the location and type of pain to a doctor can be difficult, especially for children. Remembering what the pain was like after a few weeks or months can also be hard. When each headache is a little different, this process can be even more complicated. Making sketches of headaches can be a valuable tool in understanding them. The picture could be of the face, top or back of the head, side of the head, or all of these angles, depending on the type of headache. Jagged or wiggly lines, colors, or drawings of hammers or lightning bolts might be used to represent the type and location of pain. Artistry is not important, but the record of the headache is valuable in determining how to treat migraines.

The Effects on Daily Life

Some people who experience migraines feel that the worst part of a migraine is not the pain but the effect it has on everyday life. Migraines frequently cause a person to miss work or school and then have to catch up when the migraine is over. Migraine episodes can also interfere with sports, social activities, housework, vacations, and special occasions such as weddings and graduations. With no reliable method to predict when a migraine will hit, migraine sufferers are sometimes at the mercy of their own bodies.

Allodynia

The medical definition of allodynia means "pain from stimuli which are not normally painful." In other words, allodynia refers to pain that should not be happening—pain caused by wearing clothes or taking a shower. Allodynia sometimes comes with a migraine. People prone to migraines have reported several types of allodynia, including the following:

- sensitive scalp
- sore muscles on head or neck
- pain while combing hair
- pain from cold air contacting the head
- a headache worsened by heat from a hair dryer, stove, or fireplace
- discomfort from wearing clothes
- pain from wearing jewelry

When allodynia occurs, a migraine is usually in full swing. The appearance of allodynia is generally a sign that the migraine is so far along that medication will be unable to prevent it. A study at Beth Israel Deaconess Medical Center in Boston compared early migraines with migraines that had progressed to include allodynia. Researchers discovered that the medicine sumatriptan eliminated a migraine in only five out of thirty-four cases that had reached allodynia. In patients who were given sumatriptan before allodynia could occur, the medicine worked in twenty-five out of twenty-seven cases. Rami Burstein, the physician who conducted the study, says, "We can now predict with about 90 percent accuracy whether a patient will respond to triptan before we give the drug, and we can increase the success rate from about 40 percent to over 90 percent."

MedicineNet.com, "Definition of Allodynia." www.medterms.com/script/main/art .asp?articlekey=25197.

Quoted in Tom Fagan, "Mechanism Found for Migraine Med." http://focus.hms .harvard.edu/2003/Dec12_2003/neurobiology.html.

When migraines cause people to miss work, they either lose out on wages or their employer gives them sick pay. According to the Web site CureResearch.com, migraines cause about $13 billion every year in lost wages. That amount could be as high as $29 billion per year, according to the Web site Migraine Headaches Aid. In a study of migraine patients conducted by the pharmaceutical company Merck, migraine sufferers reported losing an average of twenty work days per year. That lost work time included days when the migraine patient was at work but had difficulty functioning normally and was not working at full efficiency. Because a high number of migraines are never diagnosed, experts believe that the costs are actually much higher. The real costs could be nearly twice as much as these estimates.

Lost wages are only part of the picture. Migraine patients also suffer anxiety from missing work. They worry that missing work or low productivity could result in getting fired or being passed up for promotions or raises. They worry about what coworkers think of their illness; some people simply do not understand or do not believe that migraines are real.

Migraine sufferers also feel an impact on their social lives. Some are unable to attend activities with friends if known triggers will be present, such as odors, noises, or bright lights. Shopping, concerts, and sporting events such as auto races might offer strong migraine triggers and require someone prone to migraines to stay away. The possible onset of a migraine is constantly present and could cause someone to cancel plans for a movie, dinner, or other social activity.

Guilt is a common emotion in migraine sufferers. By missing out on activities, falling behind at work, or not accomplishing household tasks, many people feel guilt or inadequacy. Even though they know that their condition is real, and they know firsthand the severity of their pain, they still suffer from guilt at times over a physical condition that they cannot control. Parents who suffer from migraines often feel guilty when they must cancel activities with their children.

Migraine sufferers are often the targets of bad advice. This might come from a well-meaning friend or relative or an insensitive stranger or coworker. Most of the time, bad advice comes from someone who does not understand migraines or who believes a migraine is just a simple headache. Migraine sufferers might hear things like, "Just walk it off," "Take more pain medicine," "Try to push through it," or "You're just being dramatic." Statements like these do not help the person and tend to cause more anxiety and guilt. Marti Sanders, who experiences migraines, remembers dealing with an insensitive boss:

> I worked in a restaurant and I called in sick once with a migraine. I was told it would be really busy that night and I had to come in. I got dressed and went to work, but my face was white as a ghost and my hands were shaking. I was squinting the whole time because of the lights and I could barely concentrate. After about an hour, a manager looked at me and asked what was wrong. I told him I had a migraine. He said, "Oh, I thought you were faking. I didn't think anyone actually got migraines." He apologized and let me go home. I just kept hoping that he had learned a lesson.[15]

Migraines and Depression

For many years, doctors have suspected a link between migraines and depression. Bouts of depression were recognized as signals in the premonitory phase in some patients. Theories were posed that some migraine patients suffered from depression as a result of migraine pain or as a side effect of missing out on events, continually catching up, and the guilt of not accomplishing daily tasks.

A study by the Henry Ford Health System revealed a strong link between migraines and depression. Migraine sufferers were found to be five times more likely than nonsufferers to experience major depression. Patients with diagnosed depression were found to be three times more likely to develop migraines than nondepressed patients.

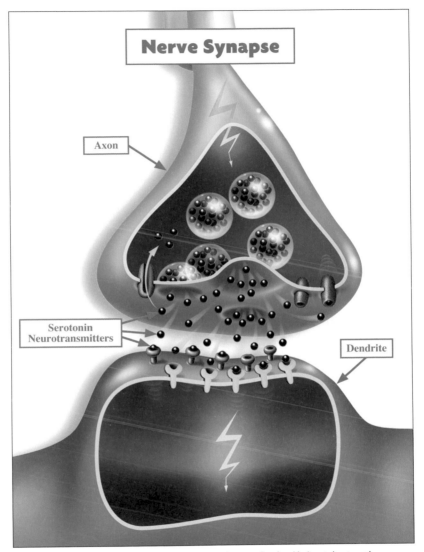

Nerve Synapse

Axon

Serotonin
Neurotransmitters

Dendrite

The neurotransmitter serotonin (purple balls) aids in the transmission of nerve impulses across nerve synapses. One theory suggests migraines are caused by the brain releasing abnormal amounts of serotonin.

In a separate study at a Canadian anxiety disorders clinic, 67 percent of patients under treatment for anxiety and depression also reported migraines. The doctors who performed that study found this link to be extraordinarily high.

The connection between migraines and depression is unclear. Theories propose that hormones or brain chemicals such as serotonin may play a part. Serotonin is a neurotransmitter—it helps the brain cells send messages. One theory about migraines is that the brain releases abnormal amounts of serotonin. New theories about depression propose that an imbalance in serotonin is a factor in depression. Thus, serotonin could be contributing to both depression and migraines at the same time.

In support of these theories, doctors also know that certain medicines used to treat depression are sometimes effective in treating migraines. Further research is needed to determine the nature of the link between migraines and depression. A question that begs to be answered is whether migraines cause depression or whether depression is the cause of migraines. One possibility is that the answer depends on the individual patient. Or, serotonin levels may simply be the cause of both conditions.

The Cost of Care

Another burden of the migraine patient is the cost of caring for this condition. The cost of doctor visits and testing is estimated at $6.2 billion per year in the United States. Prescription medicines are estimated at another $5.2 billion per year. Emergency room care and inpatient hospital care make up another $1.3 billion each year. Health insurance covers many of these costs, but not all. For some people, even though evaluation, treatment, and medicines are available, they cannot afford the expense that could provide relief from migraines.

Some insurance plans limit the number of pills a person can receive each month. This leads some people to make hard decisions about whether to take the medication. They fear that if a headache is not a migraine, they have wasted a pill. Some of these people wait to take a pill until they are certain they are getting a migraine; yet this delay can make the medication less effective or not work at all. Migraine medications can cost $21.00 to $26.00 per pill or more, and nasal sprays can cost around $32.00 per dose. Some people get several migraines per month, so the costs multiply quickly. Those costs are simply too high for some people. Because some migraine medications are very new, less expensive generic drugs are not yet available.

Research indicates that taking migraine medication in a timely manner can actually save money in the long run. When a person can take medication and avoid a migraine, he or she is less likely to lose time at work and other activities. In addition, blocking a migraine may reduce the need to visit an emergency room in the event of an extreme headache.

Helping Kids Cope with Migraines

The symptoms and severity of migraines can be frightening for adults, but they can be even more upsetting for children and teens. When a migraine hits, especially for the first time, children are scared by the extreme pain and might worry about what is happening. They might fear that they are going to die. They are likely to wonder why such a painful headache is happening to them. Miya Kressin's first migraine hit when she was eight years old. She recalls:

> I had a normal headache that lasted two or three days, and my mom gave me acetaminophen. Several days later, I got another headache that wouldn't go away. The doctor's office recommended acetaminophen, but that didn't help. After two weeks, the doctor saw me, and I had a lot of tests—an MRI, CT scan, and EEG [electroencephalogram]. They didn't find anything and could only tell me it was a migraine. They gave me prescription-strength Tylenol. That headache lasted 26 days.

> I don't have many memories of that summer. I remember the first headache vaguely and I remember being in pain, crying, lying in a dark room with a cold rag over my eyes a few times during the second migraine. Mostly I remember the hospital visits for the tests.

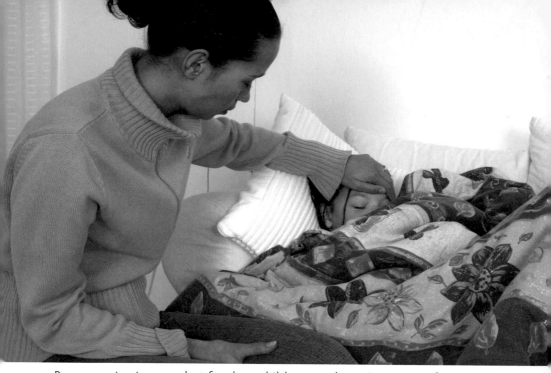

Because migraines can last for days, children need continuous comfort and reassurance from their parents to help them through the ordeal.

The doctor prescribed medication, but I still got a migraine every two or three months. Around the time I turned sixteen, I went for about two years without a migraine, and they gradually took me off the medication. I still get migraines as an adult.[16]

Children need comfort and reassurance during a headache and any doctor visits that follow. Hospitals can be strange and scary to children. Parents and caregivers should try to help the child remain calm and might suggest that the child bring a favorite stuffed animal to any doctor visits or tests.

Parents may wish to talk with teachers, coaches, or a school nurse about their child's migraines. They might explain that the headaches are real, not just an excuse to get out of school. Parents can give instructions about how to help the child when a migraine hits, such as ensuring that any medication is taken promptly or allowing the child to lie down or take other measures. A note or instructions from the child's doctor is usually helpful in explaining the situation to teachers or other adults.

Keeping a journal or drawing pictures of headaches can be especially helpful to a child. This information is useful to the doctor in understanding the headaches. It can also help relieve stress for a child by allowing a form of expression.

Children and teens should be actively involved in managing their migraines. The more young people understand about migraines, the more they can help prevent the headaches. They can watch for and avoid food and environmental triggers. This also helps the child or teen to feel more in control of his or her headaches and to feel less victimized by them. Young people can be taught to recognize the warning signs of a migraine and should thoroughly understand how to respond by taking medication or other steps to block the migraine. Ned Schnitzer's twelve-year-old son experiences migraines. "When my son got his first headache, we were scared to death," Schnitzer recalls.

We worried that he might have brain cancer or something. He was in so much pain and we were completely helpless. Finding out that he had a migraine was actually good news. He wasn't going to die. He still gets the headaches, and they're awful for him, but we know what to expect. And we know that strong smells like cigarette smoke or bus exhaust can be triggers. Those are pretty easy to avoid. He holds his breath if we run into a strong smell.[17]

Working with Medications

Because every person is unique, no medication can cure every migraine every time. Migraine patients typically go through a trial-and-error period with their doctors. A doctor will suggest medication based on the patient's symptoms and health history. The patient can then use that medication and judge its effectiveness. Some patients get lucky and have success right away. Others may find no relief at all, even after trying several drugs.

Communication with a doctor is important. When a medication is unsuccessful, the doctor should be notified so a different medication can be prescribed. The doctor should also be contacted if the medication produces unpleasant side effects, such as drowsiness, aches, inability to sleep, or jitteriness. Some patients are willing to live with mild side effects if the medication is highly effective. Other side effects may be unbearable and require a medication to be stopped.

Finding a helpful migraine medication requires patience. It may require sampling a number of different drugs to find one that works. A migraine journal can be useful in this process. By recording any changes in migraines along with any side effects, the patient and doctor can evaluate medications and find the best solution.

Rebound Headaches

Some people experience an unwelcome side effect of taking medication. Those who take pain medication more than two or three times a week sometimes suffer from a rebound headache. As their bodies become accustomed to their medication, changes in dosage or environment can cause a new headache. Doctors refer to these as medication-induced headaches or, more commonly, rebound headaches because the medication seems to bounce back at the patient and cause, rather than cure, a headache.

Rebound headaches sometimes include nausea, irritability, anxiety, or restlessness. A person who suspects trouble should contact his or her doctor and likely will need to stop taking the medication. The person may experience more headaches as his or her body adjusts, and some people require hospitalization. After the person has been freed of the effects of the medication, a new discussion with the doctor will be necessary to decide on new treatments for migraines.

Rebound headaches are not the same as drug addiction, in which the body craves a certain medication.

U.S. Headache Consortium Guidelines

Because migraines and other headaches have become a major area of study, the U.S. Headache Consortium was formed. It is a committee of doctors from the American Headache Society, the National Headache Foundation, the American College of Emergency Physicians, the American Academy of Family Physicians, and other medical groups. This group of scientists has formulated guidelines for patients and for physicians who treat headaches. These guidelines illustrate that a number of approaches might be needed in order to conquer migraines.

For migraine sufferers, the consortium recommends certain lifestyle modifications:

- Record how often headaches occur and try to identify factors that trigger them.
- Avoid triggers after they have been identified.
- Patients should locate an understanding physician who is experienced in treating headaches and is willing to work to achieve the best treatment.
- Patients should inform their doctor about the effect of headaches on daily life. A headache diary is an excellent tool for this.
- Migraines should be treated with appropriate medications—over-the-counter medications for less severe attacks, and prescription drugs for moderate to severe migraines.
- Headache medications should be used in moderation. Many can cause dependency or can cause rebound headaches if taken too frequently.
- A "rescue" medication may be kept on hand in case the regular medication does not work.
- Find the treatment that works. If a medication does not work after three subsequent migraine episodes, patients should ask their doctor to prescribe a different medication.
- Discuss preventative drugs with a doctor.
- Consider alternative therapies, such as relaxation or biofeedback, if medications are not helpful or cannot be taken.

Ancient Egyptian Medicine

The ancient Egyptians treated headaches. Their remedy was to place a clay model of a crocodile atop the patient's head. The crocodile's mouth was filled with grain and then a strip of linen bearing the names of the gods was wrapped under the patient's chin and over the head to tie the crocodile in place. Researchers believe that the pressure of the figurine and the cooling effect of the clay may have provided some relief.

Ancient Egyptians treated headaches by attaching a clay crocodile figurine (similar to the one shown) to the top of a patient's head using strips of linen.

Although migraines are difficult to live with and challenging to understand, many strategies exist to help people who suffer from them. When migraine sufferers take an active role in understanding their headaches and how they fit into their lifestyle, they have the best chance of conquering their pain. The highest success comes when a patient and doctor work as a team and communicate effectively to analyze migraines and test treatments to find the best results.

CHAPTER FOUR

Migraine Treatment

Before modern equipment like X-rays and MRIs were invented, and before discoveries such as aspirin, acetaminophen, and new prescription medicines, understanding and treating migraines was difficult. Headache sufferers had to rely on advice from friends and family, and doctors had few safe treatments they could offer. Most people depended on home remedies to treat their headache pain and other ailments.

Homemade remedies are known as folk remedies, and they consist of treatments that patients can concoct in their own kitchens with local ingredients. Some folk remedies for migraines include inhaling vinegar fumes; massaging menthol, eucalyptus oil, peppermint oil, or rosemary oil on the forehead; or consuming a tea made from cayenne pepper, celery seeds, or ginger. Soaking a person's feet in hot water containing powdered mustard is another remedy, as is eating a few teaspoons of honey at each meal. These treatments have not been scientifically tested, and estimating the success of such folk remedies is difficult. In recent times, some doctors have begun to look to folk remedies and judge whether they might have merit. They realize that in many cases, folk remedies were actually effective and could be studied for current uses.

An example of a folk remedy that is undergoing study by researchers is peppermint oil. A laboratory study using rats tested ordinary bedding and bedding that was treated with peppermint oil. The rats were given a pain stimulus. Those with peppermint oil in their bedding responded in a way that

Peppermint oil rubbed on the forehead has been shown to successfully treat tension-type headaches.

indicated their pain was less severe compared with the rats with ordinary bedding. To treat a migraine, peppermint oil is rubbed on the forehead; this remedy has shown success with tension-type headaches. Because peppermint oil has virtually no risks, it is safe for people to test and may receive further study for migraines.

With so many people suffering from migraines, cures are highly sought after. Numerous treatments have been suggested, and some of them date back hundreds of years. None of the treatments discussed in this book should be attempted without the supervision of a doctor or a trusted adult. Some treatments are appropriate for certain people but could be dangerous for others. A person's size, weight, age, allergies, and other medical conditions, such as asthma or heart disease, are all considered when a doctor recommends treatment.

An Organized Management Method

According to the National Migraine Association, patients should consider a four-way approach to migraine management. Because no single cure exists for every migraine, and because every person has different experiences, multiple approaches offer the best chance of preventing, blocking, and treating migraines. The four approaches include preventive treatment, trigger management, abortive treatment, and general pain management.

Preventive treatments might involve a number of strategies. They might include maintaining healthy blood pressure, exercising, and eating a healthy diet. Prevention can also include taking regular medications to prevent migraines from getting started. When migraines are prevented from taking hold, patients experience the least amount of pain and the best quality of life. Researchers are always looking for new methods to prevent migraines and allow patients to avoid the headaches altogether.

Trigger management involves helping migraine patients to identify some or all of the triggers that set off a migraine. Recognizing foods or activities that start a migraine and then avoiding them can be highly effective for some patients.

In the past ten to twenty years, a number of new medications have been developed that can block a migraine before it fully takes hold. These prescription drugs are known as abortive treatments. Usually in the form of pills or nasal sprays, these treatments are taken as soon as the patient recognizes the signs of a migraine. The success rates of minimizing or completely canceling a headache are very good. These treatments are most successful when taken promptly after warning signs begin. When patients wait longer, the effectiveness of the medicines is not as high. Acupuncture is also sometimes used as an abortive treatment.

Nasal spray has worked well for Murray White. "Now that I have a nasal spray to prevent my migraines, I never leave home without it. As soon as I suspect a migraine, I use the spray. I've probably blocked about 75 percent of my migraines from taking hold."[18]

General pain management is needed when a migraine begins and progresses out of control. In spite of many measures to combat migraines, full-blown migraines often start. Every day, pain management is needed for people stricken with their first

Acupuncture needles placed in a patient's forehead have been found to relieve pain from tension headaches and migraines.

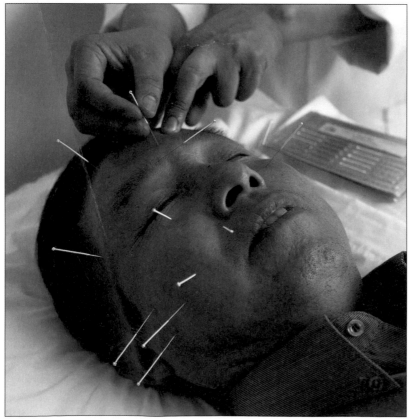

migraine. Even experienced migraine sufferers rarely prevent every migraine and must turn to pain relievers for help. Many treatments are available to lessen migraine pain, including over-the-counter medicines, prescription drugs, and other therapies.

Migraine Treatments Without Medication

Many possible treatments exist for migraines. Because migraines are so individualized, certain treatments work for some people but not for others. The best results come when a doctor and patient work together and test the various treatments. Treatments that offer no relief can be discarded, and those that lessen migraines can be followed more seriously. Most patients will test a variety of methods, ignore those that are not helpful, and incorporate those that lessen the pain or frequency of migraines.

Diet

Every day, Americans are hearing messages that a healthy diet is important for the human body to function properly. Eating fruits and vegetables, avoiding junk food, and maintaining a proper weight help to regulate blood pressure, boost the immune system, and provide energy. These steps can help a person to avoid problems such as heart disease, stroke, and diabetes. A migraine patient who follows a healthy diet improves his or her chances of successfully avoiding migraines. This includes eliminating any trigger foods from the diet.

Skipping meals is generally considered to be unhealthy, and it can sometimes bring on a migraine. This is a problem that can usually be avoided. Some patients keep healthy snacks handy in case they miss a meal. When a meal is unavoidably missed, patients usually take steps to eat as soon as possible or perhaps take medication to block a possible migraine.

The human body needs a number of specific vitamins and minerals in order to function and be healthy. Most of these are found in foods, but processed foods and fast foods tend to lose vitamins and minerals. Many migraine patients consult with a doctor to learn which vitamins or minerals are important. A doctor may recommend a multivitamin once per day or may advise other specific combinations of vitamins or minerals. Magnesium is considered especially important for people suffering from migraines, and it is found in nuts; legumes; dark green, leafy vegetables; and whole-grain foods.

Vitamin B2, also known as riboflavin, has attracted special attention recently. Studies have shown that high doses of riboflavin over a period of four months can be effective in preventing migraines. Approximately half of the patients in the studies reported improvement in their migraines. Further study is needed to determine whether riboflavin can be effective in preventing migraines in the general public.

Neil Koepke has wondered if his migraines are related to diet and changes in blood sugar. As a diabetic, he must watch his diet and monitor his blood sugar several times each day. His migraines always begin in the morning—after not eating all night, blood sugar tends to be lowest in the morning. "I usually wake up with a migraine. I usually try to fight through them. Most of the time, my medication kicks in and I am okay after about 2:00 P.M. I had a migraine during a business trip to Dallas and it prevented me from accomplishing the business task at hand."[19] Koepke is careful about what he eats, but the migraines still occur.

Hydration

Along with a healthy diet, doctors have known for many years that water is essential to good health. The human body is about 60 percent water, and the brain is about 75 percent water. Water inside the body helps in healing, eliminating wastes, and delivering nutrients to the cells. When a person does not drink enough water, dehydration sets in. This can cause stomachache, muscle cramps, headache, and dizziness. Migraine sufferers are wise to stay hydrated as a step to avoid headaches. A properly hydrated brain may be less likely to experience disturbances in the levels of brain chemicals.

Caffeine

Coffee, tea, and certain sodas contain caffeine, which is a mild stimulant. Many people look for coffee or soda in the morning to help them wake up. Caffeine has been shown to play a part in migraines, but its link is unusual—some patients consider caffeine to be a trigger, but others find it helpful in treating a headache.

Exercise

Doctors recommend exercise for nearly everyone. Walking, bike riding, swimming, and playing sports help to keep the heart and muscles healthy. For people with migraines, regular exercise can help by keeping the body in shape, regulating blood sugar, and maintaining energy.

In some patients, however, exercise can set off a migraine. Strenuous exercise, such as weight lifting, running a marathon, or pushups, could start a headache. For these patients, a migraine journal can be an important tool. By recording the types and levels of exercise and comparing them to migraine onset, patterns can be discovered. A patient can then design an exercise plan to maintain health and avoid migraines.

Sleep

Most American adults and teens do not get the amount of sleep recommended by doctors. Researchers are beginning to identify and understand the problems associated with a lack of sleep. Some people prone to migraines have discovered that too much or too little sleep can start a migraine. In order to prevent migraines, a person needs to understand his or her personal sleep requirements. Recording sleep habits in a migraine journal can help identify this relationship. When a migraine occurs, the journal can be consulted to determine whether the person has been in a pattern of too much or too little sleep. The person can then take steps to regulate sleeping habits and attempt to avoid migraines.

Stress Management

Stress is known to bring on migraines. Some people seek ways to reduce stress by staying organized, keeping lists, asking others for help, and managing the number of events in their schedules. They might also find ways to unwind from stress, such as taking a bath, listening to music, spending time with friends or family, or setting aside personal time each day. Some of the therapies listed in this section are effective at reducing stress and may be part of the reason why they are effective in reducing migraines.

Deep Breathing and Proper Posture

Although everyone knows how to breathe, physician Mehmet Oz contends that not everyone breathes correctly. When people are under stress, they sometimes unconsciously tighten abdominal muscles. Breathing becomes shallow—air is drawn from only halfway down the chest. Deep breathing can help increase oxygen in the body and bring about relaxation. Oz recommends that everyone should learn to engage in deep breathing all the way to the diaphragm, and then practice this for several minutes each day. He has demonstrated this technique on television on programs such as *Good Morning America* and *The Oprah Winfrey Show*. Deep breathing may be especially beneficial for people who suffer from migraines because it increases the flow of oxygen and brings about relaxation.

Posture is related to breathing and muscle tension. When people slouch or slump, they force the spine into abnormal positions and compress the lungs. This can result in back pain and shallow breathing. By sitting up or standing tall, with the spine straight, shoulders back, and chest forward (instead of caved in), everyone can benefit from deeper breathing and less stress on the back.

Muscle Relaxation or Massage

Tension in the muscles, particularly in the head and neck, is believed to bring on migraines for some people. Relaxation

Deep breathing exercises benefit migraine sufferers because they help increase oxygen levels and bring about relaxation.

techniques can help people learn to release tension when they are under stress and thus avoid migraines.

Massage is also known to relieve muscle tension. Some people seek out a full massage from a professional, but others learn simple techniques they can practice on themselves, such as massaging the head and neck.

Biofeedback

The term *biofeedback* refers to the theory that humans can be taught to control involuntary body mechanisms. This practice requires professional training and demands time and patience. To learn biofeedback, a person is fitted with sensors that monitor heart rate, breathing, and blood pressure. By engaging in several techniques, a person can learn to regulate blood pressure, skin temperature, and heart rate. In addition to providing relaxation, biofeedback can sometimes be used to slow or block the early stages of a migraine. This technique requires months or years to learn and is not a quick fix for migraines. Not all patients who attempt to learn biofeedback are successful.

Acupuncture

Practiced for centuries in China, acupuncture is a technique in which tiny needles—some only as thick as a human hair—are inserted into the skin at key locations. The process is said to free the passage of energy—known as chi—that flows through the body. Many people claim to experience relief from acupuncture for conditions such as arthritis, back pain, menstrual cramps, and even migraines.

Miya Kressin has had favorable results in relieving her migraines after acupuncture. Hoping to get some relief from fluid retention, she visited an acupuncturist. After several visits she noticed that her migraines were not coming as often. Kressin relates, "I told my acupuncturist that my migraines had gotten better. He said, 'Why didn't you tell me you had migraines?' He adjusted my treatments and I could see immediate results. Now, when I feel a migraine coming on, I get to him as quickly as possible. By inserting only three needles in my forehead, he can either block a migraine entirely or reduce the pain level."[20]

Yoga and Tai Chi

Yoga is an ancient system of exercise that originated in India and incorporates breathing and meditation. Yoga involves moving the body into various poses. The body benefits from

Yoga, an ancient system of exercise that incorporates breathing techniques and meditation, has been found to be effective in reducing tension headaches and migraines.

stretching and gaining flexibility. Muscles are also exercised while holding a yoga pose; when a participant works to maintain balance in the pose, the muscles must work to hold the body in place. Yoga is considered a low-impact workout because it does not stress the joints.

Tai chi is a martial art from China. It also places emphasis on breathing, balance, and meditation. It has been described as "moving yoga" because it involves working the body through a series of established poses. It is low impact and easy on joints, such as knees and elbows. Tai chi also offers flexibility and stretching.

Both of these exercises can be beneficial to migraine sufferers. Because they are gentle exercise, they avoid bringing on headaches the way strenuous exercise, such as running or weight lifting, can. Some patients report that yoga or tai chi helps them to relax from stress and thus reduce the chance of getting a migraine.

Physical Therapy

People with weak muscles, physical abnormalities, or who have experienced migraines following an accident may find relief with physical therapy. A licensed physical therapist can help to strengthen, stretch, or relax muscles, especially in the neck and shoulders. Physical therapists are trained to analyze the way muscles move and identify problems with strength, posture, and symmetry. They can teach a patient exercises that will correct any number of problems with the muscles or skeleton. Correcting certain physical problems can sometimes help relieve migraines.

Support Groups

People who experience migraines deal not only with pain but also with the guilt and frustration of missing activities or work because of their headaches. Some hospitals offer support groups for migraine sufferers. These groups help people to deal with their feelings by sharing their stories, advice, and worries with others in the same situation.

Medication for Migraines

Several medicines currently exist for treating migraines. Some of these can be purchased in a drug store or grocery store. Others require a prescription from a doctor. All medications carry certain risks, so children under age eighteen should never take medicines without the permission of a parent, doctor, or trusted adult. Selecting a medication can be tricky and depends on a person's other health factors.

Aspirin

Described by doctors as "the wonder drug," aspirin can relieve pain and swelling. It is also a blood thinner, which means it reduces the blood's ability to clot. Aspirin is sometimes recommended to prevent strokes or heart attacks. Some migraine sufferers take aspirin to relieve pain; they sometimes combine it with caffeine. Doctors believe that aspirin may even hold hidden benefits that have not yet been discovered.

Because it is a blood thinner, aspirin must be avoided by anyone who has had recent surgery or has a clotting disorder.

It should not be taken by children or teens who have viral illnesses due to the risk of developing Reye's syndrome, a potentially fatal complication. When taken safely in the absence of these situations, some people prone to migraines find adequate relief by taking aspirin.

Acetaminophen

Commonly known by the brand name Tylenol, acetaminophen is a popular medicine for relieving pain and lowering fever. Acetaminophen is available in liquid form for infants,

Reye's Syndrome

Reye's syndrome is a deadly disease that can follow a viral illness, such as the flu or chicken pox, and affects people of all ages. It typically develops as a person is recovering from a virus, and it affects the liver and brain. Symptoms include continuous vomiting, listlessness, delirium, extreme sleepiness, and confusion. Reye's syndrome is not contagious and is not related to migraines.

The U.S. Food and Drug Administration, the Centers for Disease Control and Prevention, and the American Academy of Pediatrics recommend that aspirin should not be taken by anyone under nineteen years of age during fever-causing illnesses. If a fever is present or a virus is suspected, aspirin is not recommended. Aspirin use in children has been linked to death from Reye's syndrome when taken during the flu or for other viruses.

The use of aspirin for migraine treatment in children and teens should be approached with caution. A discussion with a trusted doctor can help determine the best choice of treatment.

For more information, refer to the National Reye's Syndrome Foundation, which can be found online at www.reyessyndrome .org/index.html.

Acetaminophen Risks

The pain reliever acetaminophen, which is the active ingredient in the medicine Tylenol and other brands, poses a risk of liver damage when taken in high doses. Consumers sometimes fail to follow dosing instructions on the packaging, believing that the medicine is safe in any dose. Some patients forget that the medicine should be taken only for a recommended number of days.

Patients sometimes unknowingly overdose on acetaminophen. Consumers taking cold medicines containing acetaminophen sometimes also take plain acetaminophen to relieve pain. They are unaware that they are taking two products with acetaminophen.

In 2009 the U.S. Food and Drug Administration issued new warnings about appropriate doses of acetaminophen. It required that manufacturers include warnings about liver damage on packaging. This rule is intended to alert consumers to the risk of taking too much acetaminophen. People who regularly use acetaminophen to treat their migraines should check with their doctor frequently and ensure that they are within safe limits.

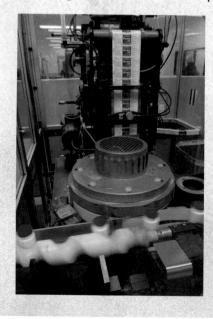

In compliance with a 2009 U.S. Food and Drug Administration regulation, acetaminophen package labels must carry warnings about the risk of liver damage that may occur through overuse of the drug.

chewable tablets for children, and higher-strength pills for teens and adults. Acetaminophen reduces headache pain in some migraine sufferers. It is available in drug, grocery, and discount stores without a prescription. It is combined with stronger medications in the prescription pain relievers Vicodin and Percocet.

Acetaminophen is generally considered to be safe in the correct doses. Patients who consume extremely high doses of acetaminophen run the risk of liver damage, which can be fatal.

Ibuprofen

Sold under the brand names Advil and Motrin, ibuprofen is a popular remedy for headaches, body aches, and fevers. It was once available only by prescription, but it is currently available over the counter in drug, grocery, and discount stores. Like aspirin, ibuprofen is favored for its ability to reduce inflammation and swelling.

Many migraine sufferers use ibuprofen to treat their headaches. "If I can take enough ibuprofen quickly, as soon as I recognize a migraine, I can usually reduce the headache to a point that I can function,"[21] says Deborah Weaver, who suffers from migraines. Other people with moderate migraines report similar success when ibuprofen is taken early. Current research shows that for some people, ibuprofen is more effective when taken with caffeine.

Ergotamine Medications

In 1938 ergotamine was found to be effective in relieving migraine pain. Ergotamine had been known since ancient Greek and Roman times, when it was used for a variety of medicinal purposes. In 1853 ergotamine was identified as a fungus that grows on wheat and bread.

Currently, ergotamine is still used as a pain medication in several forms and under several brand names. It is also used as a nasal spray, which allows the medicine to be absorbed quickly by the patient, making it a good choice for an abortive drug. During Terrell Davis's famous migraine during Super Bowl XXXII, he used an ergotamine nasal spray that allowed him to get back in the game.

Triptans

A category of drug known as triptans is designed to control the behavior of serotonin. Triptans are available in about seven different forms. The most commonly used form is called sumatriptan, and it has become the most extensively studied medication in the history of migraines. Triptans are effective in relieving headaches, photophobia, phonophobia, and nausea, and they help enable patients to engage in normal activities. Triptans continue to be researched, and new forms are being developed and tested.

Combination Medications

When a single medicine fails to have an effect on migraines, some doctors turn to combination medicines. Aspirin and acetaminophen, for example, can be purchased in combination without a prescription, sometimes with caffeine added. This product is sometimes labeled specifically as a migraine medication.

With a doctor's prescription, acetaminophen and other drugs are available combined with codeine and other pain relievers. Some well-known names are Vicodin and Percocet. Morphine-based medicines are also sometimes used.

Numerous combination medications are available by prescription. Before prescribing them for a patient, a doctor must consider the patient's other health issues. These medications have the potential to become addictive, so doctors and patients must watch for signs of dependency and take steps to prevent addiction.

Medications for Blood Pressure

Two types of medications intended to treat high blood pressure (also called hypertension) have been successful in treating migraines. One of these is called a beta blocker and is available in about five different forms under various brand names. Beta blockers help regulate the heartbeat and dilate the blood vessels. They have a wide range of minor side effects.

The other hypertension medication that is effective for migraines is the calcium channel blocker. It also comes in different forms under several brand names. Calcium channel blockers work to slow a fast heartbeat and dilate the arteries, which lowers blood pressure. Calcium channel blockers have fewer side effects than beta blockers.

Both of these medications have been successful in reducing the number of migraines that patients suffer. Doctors and patients need to work closely to gauge the effectiveness of the medication and discuss any side effects as well as monitor blood pressure and heart health.

Neurotoxins

A recent development in the treatment of migraines is the use of neurotoxins. A neurotoxin is a substance that causes damage to the nerves or tissues. In the case of migraines, a neurotoxin known by the brand name Botox is used. Botox is derived from the botulinum toxin, more commonly known as a food poisoning called botulism. Food poisoning from botulism can be fatal.

When Botox is injected into the body, it weakens or paralyzes muscles. It is most commonly known as a treatment for facial wrinkles—by paralyzing certain muscles in the face, wrinkles are less noticeable. Botox has also been used for other medical conditions. The use of Botox for migraines was discovered accidentally. People who received Botox injections reported that their migraine symptoms were lessened.

For treatment of migraines, Botox is injected into the muscles above the brow, across the forehead, around the eyes, on the sides of the head, and on the back of the head near the neck. Doctors are still studying this procedure to determine the most effective injection sites. Botox injections last for three to four months and then must be

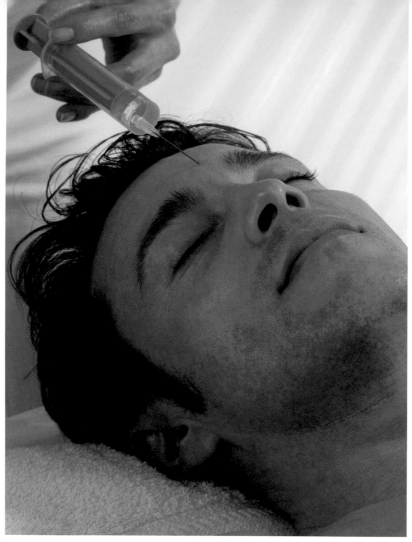

A man receives a neurotoxin injection of Botox in the front of his forehead to relieve migraine pain.

repeated. Researchers are trying to understand the link between this treatment and the success in relieving migraines.

Antidepressants

Although antidepressants are intended to relieve depression and prevent mood swings, several are also prescribed to prevent migraines. The different types of antidepressants that are available affect different mechanisms inside the brain. Some of these mechanisms regulate serotonin. Tricyclic antidepressants are currently considered to be the most effective at preventing migraines. Yet despite their success with migraine relief, some of these medications have a number of side effects, including dry mouth, drowsiness, and increased appetite. The use of antidepressants must be considered carefully in migraine patients. The link between migraines and depression is currently an area of high interest for further study.

Anti-Seizure Medications

Some migraine patients have found relief from their headaches by taking anti-seizure medicines. A seizure is a disturbance in the brain that causes abnormal behavior. Seizures can range from short blackouts to episodes of uncontrolled kicking and thrashing, and can be dangerous. Seizures can be caused by several different conditions, including a disorder called epilepsy, which brings on frequent seizures. Migraines are not considered to be related to seizures.

Certain medications are used to control epilepsy and other seizures. These medications help prevent neurotransmitters in the brain from over-firing. Two specific medications—topiramate and divalproex sodium—are currently approved for migraine patients. These medicines are taken daily and have reduced the frequency of migraines for some patients. These types of drugs are more expensive than other migraine medications. In addition, they can cause serious side effects. Divalproex sodium cannot be taken by pregnant women due to a risk of birth defects.

Several other anti-seizure medications are currently being studied for possible treatment of migraines.

Putting the Puzzle Together

Migraines are like an enormous puzzle. Their wide range of different symptoms must first be analyzed to see the picture of a migraine. Then, by experimenting with various lifestyle techniques and medications, a doctor and patient can start to sort the pieces into a reasonable order. Sometimes, pieces have to be thrown away entirely, or pieces are missing from the scene. Patience and persistence are two of the most important tools when trying to understand migraines and prevent their return.

CHAPTER FIVE

The Future of Migraines

Although migraines have become accepted as a neurological disease, they are still misunderstood by doctors, migraine sufferers, and the general public. Many migraine specialists realize the difficulties they face.

Joel Saper, a neurologist with the Michigan Headache and Neurological Institute in Ann Arbor, encounters this problem. He expressed his gratitude to the Migraine Research Foundation, which was founded in 2007, for its role in encouraging and funding migraine research. "Migraine is under-researched by the scientific community, under-treated by physicians, and under-appreciated by society," says Saper. "There is no condition of such magnitude, yet so shrouded in myth, misinformation, and mistreatment, as migraine. The Migraine Research Foundation is about more than just the research that it will fund directly—it is about stimulating others to join us in addressing a critical gap in medical research."[22] Researchers are getting closer to understanding the causes of migraines. When that discovery is eventually made, new methods of treatment are likely to follow quickly. At some point, a "miracle pill" may even be discovered that can prevent migraines altogether.

William B. Young and Stephen D. Silberstein, neurologists with the Jefferson Headache Center in Philadelphia, understand the research opportunities that lie ahead. "We are at the threshold of an explosion in the understanding, diagnosis, and treatment of migraine and other headaches. Many new treatments have been developed, and many more are in various stages of development. [Along] with this is the renewed dedication of clinicians to headache treatment and teaching."[23]

Many different kinds of migraine research are under way at any given time. Research might focus on the causes, triggers, or process of migraines, the prevention of migraines, or ways to halt migraines that have begun. The field of migraine research is extremely broad, but any area of research could provide a breakthrough at any time.

New Conclusions About Migraines

The great amount of migraine research that is continually under way means that new theories are always developing. As a result of new information, many experts now agree that

These thermogram pictures of a migraine sufferer's head show the onset of a migraine, left, and after, right. The white areas show hot spots in the brain and neck caused by the migraine.

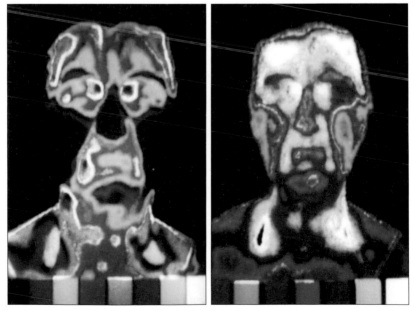

migraine-prone brains differ from brains that do not experience migraines. Migraine-prone brains are described as hyperexcitable. As Carolyn Bernstein, a physician who specializes in headache treatment, explains, "It's a brain that's more sensitive than the brain of someone who doesn't have migraines. Cells in the brain of a person with migraines tend to get irritated or excited and begin to send off signals when they shouldn't, whereas the brain of someone who doesn't have migraines probably wouldn't react."[24]

Researchers also hope to understand the link between migraines and depression. Because serotonin plays a part in both disorders, the link makes sense to doctors. Understanding the serotonin mechanism may lead to better understanding of both migraines and depression.

New Testing Methods

Modern testing that allows doctors to see inside the body is critical to migraine research. The MRI, CT scan, and even X-rays allow researchers to learn more about what a migraine is and what it is not. Newer tests that may impact migraine research are also in development.

The single-photon emission computerized tomography (SPECT) scan is a modern test that lets doctors watch the function of internal organs. In this test, a patient consumes a radioactive substance; as that substance travels through the body, doctors can scan and record the behavior of organs.

Observation of the brain during a SPECT scan can help diagnose Alzheimer's disease, strokes, and seizures. SPECT scans are especially good at mapping the blood supply inside the brain; the radioactive material remains in the blood and does not enter the tissues in the brain. A SPECT scan can help diagnose migraines by ruling out other possible conditions. SPECT scans may also help future research.

Experimental Procedures

Finding a miracle treatment for any disease takes time. Even when new treatments are proposed, they must be studied and tested. Test subjects must be located with the correct sets of symptoms, and they must be healthy enough to attempt a new treatment. Patients who undergo new treatments must be monitored to gauge the success of the treatment, watched for any side effects, and followed to learn of any long-term effects. For a treatment to become recognized and accepted, it also needs to gain the approval of the U.S. Food and Drug Administration.

Occipital Nerve Stimulation

The procedure known as occipital nerve stimulation is very new in the treatment of chronic migraines. As of early 2009, this technique was being performed in clinical testing, but it was not yet available to the general public. Test patients were reporting good results in reducing or eliminating migraines.

In this procedure, a surgeon implants a small device at the base of the skull, near the occipital nerve. Special wires are threaded under the skin to connect this device to a pacemaker. The pacemaker is also implanted under the skin, generally under the collar bone, at the lower back, or in the lower abdomen. The pacemaker sends electrical impulses to the occipital nerve. These pulses might be sent in a steady stream or as needed.

Occipital nerve stimulation has improved headaches for about 70 percent of people who have tried it. However, tests have been done only in very small numbers, and long-term results are not available. Occipital nerve stimulation requires surgery and comes with a risk of infection. In some cases, the implanted wires must be replaced or adjusted. More studies are needed before this procedure can become a common headache treatment.

Hyperbaric Oxygen Therapy

The hyperbaric chamber is perhaps best known as a treatment for scuba diving accidents that involve rapid decompression, more commonly called "the bends." Hyperbaric chambers are also used in cases of smoke inhalation and carbon monoxide poisoning. A patient is placed inside the chamber, and then the chamber is filled with pure oxygen under pressure.

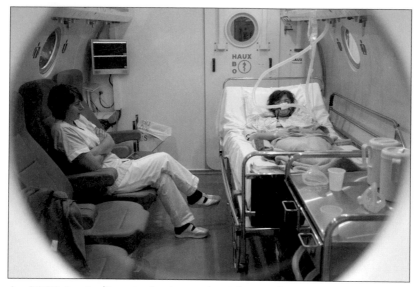

An 2009 Australian study showed evidence that treatment in a
hyperbaric oxygen chamber may relieve migraine symptoms. More
research is needed.

An Australian study published in 2009 showed evidence that
hyperbaric oxygen therapy may relieve migraine symptoms.
This treatment has drawbacks; it is not covered by health insurance, and sessions can cost approximately $250. The treat-
ment must be administered within ten to fifteen minutes of the
first symptoms in order to be effective. Hyperbaric chambers
are not common, and patients are likely to have difficulty
reaching a chamber within such a short time frame. This treatment may undergo further study, but it does not appear to be
readily available in the near future.

Transcranial Magnetic Stimulation

In April 2009 the results of transcranial magnetic stimulation
(TMS) tests were released by the University of California, San
Francisco Medical Center. Researchers found that administer-
ing magnetic pulses to migraine sufferers appeared to stop
the wave of neuron excitation that is believed to lead off a migraine. The magnetic pulses stopped the neuron wave in more
than 50 percent of patients.

TMS involves placing a large electromagnet against the patient's head. The magnet sends painless electric currents through the brain. TMS is mostly experimental and exists in only a few places across the world. Currently, it is available mostly through clinical trials. It was first devised as a treatment for depression in patients who had no success with medications or other treatments.

TMS requires a series of half-hour-long treatments several times per week over several weeks or a full month. The effects are believed to be temporary and may last only a few weeks or months. TMS comes with side effects, including headaches, scalp discomfort, twitchy facial muscles, or lightheadedness.

The outcome of TMS and its effects on both depression and migraines supports the idea that these two conditions are linked. Researchers are currently studying TMS as a treatment for a number of brain disorders.

In Transcranial Magnetic Stimulation (TMS), an electromagnet is placed around the head and sends an electric current to the brain. The current stops the neuron excitation that is believed to cause migraines.

Plastic Surgery

In 2009 the medical journal *Plastic and Reconstructive Surgery* issued the results of a study that used plastic surgery as a treatment for migraines. In the study, migraine patients underwent a forehead lift to see if their migraines improved. More than 80 percent of patients found that their migraines occurred less often following surgery. Some had only half as many headaches, and others had fewer or even no headaches at all after the surgery.

This study came about due to the observations of plastic surgeons that their patients reported fewer migraines after forehead lifts. The study offers scientific proof that this type of surgery improves migraines. Neurologists were skeptical at first, but interested. Because migraines are believed to occur deep inside the brain, success with forehead surgery did not make sense. The results of this study show that the surgery is effective, even though the mechanism is not understood.

Research into this procedure is ongoing. Doctors are excited about the potential of treating migraines through a single surgery, freeing patients from the expense and burden of taking a number of medications. They caution, however, that the surgery is not for everyone and that patients will need to meet certain standards in order to be considered for this technique.

New Drug Therapies

Doctors and researchers never know where or when the next major medical breakthrough will occur. Although new procedures or implants may show promise for migraines, traditional treatments in the form of medications are far from being abandoned. As more is understood about the mechanism of migraines, researchers can target more specific effects inside the brain. Researchers also sometimes revisit older or abandoned therapies to find out whether new information might make older therapies worth a second look.

Muscle Relaxants

Muscle relaxants have been used to treat migraines for decades, and their popularity rises and falls. Some current research is

Generic Drugs

Pharmaceutical companies spend a great deal of time and money on drug research. When a new drug is discovered, the company applies for a U.S. patent. A patent identifies the company as the owner and inventor of that drug. It also prevents other companies from producing that drug for twenty years. An example is a prescription drug called Imitrex, which is used to treat migraines.

When a new prescription drug becomes available in pharmacies, it is generally expensive at first. Pharmaceutical companies price a new drug to pay for the research that discovered and tested it. The price also includes advertising and information needed to launch the new drug.

After a few years, the price of a drug usually goes down slightly. When a drug's patent expires after twenty years, other companies may begin manufacturing and selling that drug. These companies may not use the same brand name as the company that invented it. Instead, they must use the chemical name of the drug. In the case of Imitrex, the chemical name is sumatriptan.

When a drug is sold by another company under the chemical name, it is called a generic drug. It must have the same chemical formula and properties as the original drug. When more companies begin selling the same drug, the price generally comes down due to competition for sales. The result is a savings to the consumer.

again looking at muscle relaxants. By relaxing muscles in the head and neck, headache pain is sometimes lessened. Recent studies involving a new muscle relaxant are showing this new medication to be effective in preventing tension-type headaches and migraines.

MAP0004

A medication called dihydroergotamine (DHE) is an approved drug for treating severe migraines. Research is under way to develop a new method for patients to take this medication through an inhaler. Early studies reveal that the drug can provide pain relief in only ten minutes, and it can prevent headaches for at least twenty-four hours. "DHE is a compound that basically stops the propagation of the pain," says neurologist Paul Winner, one of the researchers in the ongoing study. "It puts the genie back in the bottle."[25]

This new treatment, called MAP0004, targets many receptors that cause migraines. It has been shown to stop all of the symptoms associated with a migraine attack, including nausea, light and sound sensitivity, and pain. Although some medications are less effective as a migraine progresses, Winner says that this new drug form can be administered at any time during a migraine, making it an especially beneficial treatment.

CGRP Receptor Antagonists

The full name of this new type of drug is calcitonin generelated peptide (CGRP) receptor antagonist. It is a very long term that means that this medication works inside the brain, at the location where blood vessels meet nerves. This medication functions to prevent blood vessels from swelling, and it also targets a pathway that carries pain information to the brain. This type of drug may help to normalize conditions inside the brain.

These drugs are still being tested. They are considered safer than triptans, another migraine medication, because they do not constrict blood vessels. They may also control pain for a longer time period than other medications. Richard Lipton, a neurologist and professor who specializes in headache research, believes that this migraine treatment shows a great deal of promise. "Many advances in migraine therapy for much of the last 18 years have been developing new triptans and new ways of delivering triptans. This is the first novel pharmacologic mechanism in decades,"[26] he says.

The first CGRP receptor antagonist to be studied is called telcagepant. In a study of nearly fourteen hundred people conducted by the Mayo Clinic in 2007 and 2009, telcagepant

Triptan drug and delivery systems, such as Imigran's sumatriptan, which is administered by an injector (right) has been found effective in treating migraines.

showed promise for relieving migraine pain. The medication relieved headaches as well as a popular migraine drug that was also part of the study, but patients reported a low rate of side effects. The new drug blocks the action of certain brain proteins that are thought to affect migraines.

This drug may be helpful to patients who have heart disease. Certain current migraine medications cannot be used by patients with heart disease because they affect the blood vessels and could cause problems in those patients.

Help for Pediatric Migraines

In March 2009 the Migraine Research Foundation announced a new plan to encourage research into migraines in children. Its new plan, called For Our Children, was designed to provide grant money for pediatric migraine research. It also established a research award for success in pediatric migraine research and a fellowship to encourage new doctors to enter this field of research. Neurologist Joel Saper expresses optimism about the new initiative: "While research in adult migraine is grossly under-funded, the study of migraine in children has been almost completely neglected. In fact, many people are completely unaware that children suffer from migraine. Also, pharmacological treatment geared toward this younger population is rarely investigated, and physicians struggle with adapting adult treatments to kids."[27]

Linking Migraines to Other Diseases

As research progresses, accidental discoveries are sometimes made or unexpected results are discovered. Some of these discoveries are linked to other diseases.

Several studies in 2008 and 2009 showed that women who get migraines experience a 30 percent lower risk for breast cancer. Researchers cannot explain the connection yet. One theory is that the pain medications used for migraines somehow lower the risk of breast cancer. On the other hand, another theory proposes that the hormone estrogen plays a role because estrogen is known to be a migraine trigger. Doctors admit that the relationship is complicated, and they are cautious about making conclusions about this link.

Researchers are also studying a correlation between migraines, strokes, and heart attacks. A report published in the June 2009 issue of *Neurology* describes an increased risk of heart attacks and strokes among women who get infrequent migraines. Tobias Kurth, the lead author of the study, cautions women prone to migraines not to panic. He explains that the findings are complex and are not yet fully understood. Further studies may provide additional information explaining this link.

Belly Fat Linked to Migraines

For the first time, a link between waist size and migraines has been discovered. In a 2009 study at Philadelphia's Drexel University College of Medicine, data from more than twenty-two thousand participants was examined. Researchers discovered that excess belly fat was associated with migraine activity.

Migraines and PFO

New research has linked migraines to a condition called patent foramen ovale (PFO). PFO is a hole between the right and left atria of the heart. In most people, this hole closes shortly after birth, but in some people, the heart wall never closes completely. The condition is not life threatening, and some people do not know they have it.

Surgical procedures can close a PFO. This is done for specific health reasons. Some patients who have had surgical closure of PFO report that their migraine pain was reduced, the migraines were less frequent, or the migraines stopped completely.

Researchers do not understand the connection between PFO and migraines. Future studies may reveal more about this link.

The increased presence of migraines was noted in men and women between the ages of twenty and fifty-five. Women with excess belly fat were 30 percent more likely to experience migraines than women with average waistlines. The increase for migraines in men was not as great. Neurologist Stephen D. Silberstein notes that the findings raise a great number of questions. He also points out that this is the first study to predict a higher occurrence of migraines in a population.

A True Migraine Cure

A true cure for migraines would be able to block every migraine episode or prevent every migraine from getting started. Doctors know that such a cure is still far off. Advances in understanding the brain have provided valuable information about migraines and have offered new treatments that aid millions of migraine sufferers. Migraines are extremely complex and are mysteriously linked to other conditions in the brain. Perhaps when all of these mysteries are unraveled, migraines will become only memories.

Notes

Introduction: A Nightmare Headache

1. Sabrina Hoffmann, interview by author, December 4, 2009.

Chapter One: A Headache or a Migraine?

2. Leslie Andrich, interview by author, July 1, 2009.
3. Miya Kressin, interview by author, July 14, 2009.
4. Kressin, interview.

Chapter Two: The Characteristics of Migraines

5. Quoted in Medical News Today, "Breakthrough in Migraine Genetics." www.medicalnewstoday.com/articles/104589.php.
6. Quoted in Migraine Awareness Group, "Migraines: Myth vs. Reality." www.migraines.org/myth/mythreal.htm.
7. Deborah Weaver, interview by author, July 2, 2009.
8. Weaver, interview.
9. Robyn Sanicki, interview by author, June 30, 2009.
10. Nancy Mildebrandt, interview by author, July 18, 2009.
11. Marilyn Hartman, interview by author, July 19, 2009.
12. Mildebrandt, interview.

Chapter Three: The Migraine Lifestyle

13. Quoted in NFL, "NFL Films Presents Top Ten Gutsiest Performances: Terrell Davis." www.nfl.com/videos/nfl-films-presents/09000d5d810a5972/Top-Ten-Gutsiest-Performances-Terrell-Davis.
14. Wayne Hoffmann, interview by author, August 20, 2009.
15. Marti Sanders, interview by author, September 24, 2009.
16. Kressin, interview.
17. Ned Schnitzer, interview by author, September 29, 2009.

Chapter Four: Migraine Treatment

18. Murray White, interview by author, October 2, 2009.
19. Neil Koepke, interview by author, October 2, 2009.
20. Kressin, interview.
21. Weaver, interview.

Chapter Five: The Future of Migraines

22. Joel Saper, "Migraine Research Foundation Launches with Announcement of First Annual Research Grants." http://stanford.wellsphere.com/migraine-headaches-article/great-news-from-the-migraine-research-foundation/212789.
23. William B. Young and Stephen D. Silberstein, *Migraine and Other Headaches*. New York: Demos Medical, 2004, p. 18.
24. Quoted in Barbara Kantrowitz and Pat Wingert, "Headaches from Hell: How Migraines Affect the Brain and Why Women Suffer More," *Newsweek*, September 16, 2008. www.newsweek.com/id/159233/page/2.
25. Quoted in Kirsten Houmann, "Migraines: New Research, New Hope," Ivanhoe.com. www.ivanhoe.com/channels/p_channelstory.cfm?storyid=20553.
26. Quoted in Houmann, "Migraines."
27. Quoted in Medical News Today, "Pediatric Migraine: New Initiative to Support Research." www.medicalnewstoday.com/articles/143222.php.

Glossary

aneurysm: An abnormal swelling or ballooning of an artery wall caused by disease or weakness.

aura: A disturbance in vision commonly experienced by migraine patients. It may include bright flashes, sparkling lines or zigzags, or blind spots.

chi: A Chinese word used to describe the natural energy of the universe. In Chinese medicine, chi is believed to flow through the body.

clinical trial: A testing procedure to study the effectiveness and side effects of a new drug or medical treatment.

constriction: The narrowing or compression of a blood vessel.

dehydration: The loss of water from the body due to sweating and/or lack of fluid consumption.

diagnosis: A doctor's assessment and identification of a patient's illness or injury.

dilation: The widening of a blood vessel.

inflammation: An increase in blood flow to tissues, which causes swelling and pain.

menopause: The process women experience when their menstrual cycle ceases.

nausea: Stomach upset that leads to the feeling that vomiting is likely.

over-the-counter medicine: A medication that can be purchased without a doctor's prescription.

prognosis: An estimate of the outcome of a patient's condition; a judgment of how well and how soon a patient might recover.

puberty: The time period in which children mature physically and girls begin menstruation.

scotoma: A blind or dark spot in the visual field that can be brought on by a migraine.

stroke: An event inside the brain that can cause disability or death. A stroke can be a blockage within a blood vessel that deprives part of the brain of oxygen, or it can be bleeding inside the brain.

symptom: A physical change in the body due to illness that can help identify the illness.

trepanation: A procedure in which a hole is drilled into the skull of a living subject. The motives for this procedure are unclear.

Organizations to Contact

American Headache Society

19 Mantua Rd.
Mt. Royal, NJ 08061
(856) 423-0043
www.achenet.org

The society's Web site offers educational information for headache sufferers, including migraine management, journaling, trigger avoidance, and recent research.

American Pain Foundation

201 N. Charles St., Ste. 710
Baltimore, MD 21201-4111
(888) 615-7246
www.painfoundation.org

The foundation is devoted to educational information and management for all types of pain. Its Web site offers an online library and a searchable list to find local support groups and resources.

Migraine Awareness Group: A National Understanding for Migraineurs (MAGNUM)

100 N. Union St., Ste. B
Alexandria, VA 22314
(703) 349-1929
www.migraines.org

Also known as the National Migraine Association, MAGNUM offers information and links about all aspects of migraines. An online community is available to allow chat among migraine sufferers. The group's Web site offers many helpful hints and posts recent developments in migraine research.

National Headache Foundation

820 N. Orleans St., Ste. 217
Chicago, IL 60610
(888) 643-5552
www.headaches.org

The foundation's Web site offers information, blogs, posts about clinical trials, and general information to help manage migraines.

For Further Reading

Books

David Buchholz, *Heal Your Headache*. New York: Workman, 2002. This book provides a doctor's tips for dealing with headaches through diet, exercise, and lifestyle.

Paula Ford-Martin, *The Everything Health Guide to Migraines*. Avon, MA: Adams Media, 2008. This guidebook helps readers to understand and deal with migraines; it is written in language for ordinary people, not just physicians.

Alexander Mauskop and Barry Fox, *What Your Doctor May Not Tell You About Migraines*. New York: Wellness Central, 2001. This book offers lifestyle techniques for migraine sufferers, many of which are outside of the ordinary realm of prescription medications.

Barbara Moe, *Everything You Need to Know About Migraines and Other Headaches*. New York: Rosen, 2000. This is an easy-to-read reference about understanding the process and treatment of migraines.

Teri Robert, *Living Well with Migraine Disease and Headache*. New York: HarperCollins, 2005. The author provides tips to make life easier for those suffering from migraines.

Diane Stafford and Jennifer Shoquist, *Migraines for Dummies*. Hoboken, NJ: Wiley, 2003. This book is a plain-English description of life with migraines and ways to cope.

Andrea Votava, *Coping with Migraines and Other Headaches*. New York: Rosen, 1997. This commonsense guide for teens helps them to understand and cope with their own headaches as well as those of family members.

Web Sites

Family Doctor (http://familydoctor.org/online/famdocen/home/children/parents/common/common/757.html). This plain-language Web site is devoted to family health issues. The migraine pages offer instructional video clips.

KidsHealth (http://kidshealth.org/kid/ill_injure/aches/ migraines.html). This Web site has different areas for parents, kids, and teens and explains how the human body works and how to stay healthy.

Mayo Clinic (www.mayoclinic.com/health/migraine-headache/DS00120). The highly respected Mayo Clinic maintains this site, which explains various medical matters in everyday language and includes a question-and-answer section.

Migraine Auras: Unpleasant or Beautiful? (Migraine #2) (http://video.aol.ca/video-detail/migraine-auras-unpleasant-or-beautiful-migraine-2/1004136870/?icid=VIDURVHTS06). This video features neurologist Stephen D. Silberstein and explains and illustrates migraine auras.

Migraine4Kids.org (www.migraine4kids.org.uk/Index.htm). Designed specifically for children and teens, this Web site offers information along with suggestions about how to cope with migraines. It is one of the few sites to discuss how children feel about their migraines.

Migraine Triggers (Health Guru Tip) http://www.5min .com/Video/What-Triggers-a-Migraine-29161323 This video, also featuring Stephen D. Silberstein, offers tips for keeping a migraine journal.

Relieve-Migraine-Headache.com (www.relieve-migraineheadache.com/index.html). This Web site is devoted to understanding and treating headaches. Articles are written in plain language and are understandable to the nonmedical community.

Index

Picture Credits

About the Author

Anne K. Brown has been writing and editing for more than twenty years. Her past work has included role-playing games, fantasy fiction, nonfiction, magazine articles, business documents, and grant writing. She especially enjoys the research aspects of her projects. Her work on this book led to a greater understanding of her own migraines. This is her seventh book.

Brown has a bachelor's degree in communication from the University of Wisconsin–Milwaukee and lives in the Milwaukee area with her husband, two daughters, and a spoiled black cat. Her family makes a hobby of visiting Wisconsin state parks and taking cave tours across the country.

She is pleased that Terrell Davis succeeded in conquering his migraine during Super Bowl XXXII, but was disappointed that it allowed the Broncos to defeat the Green Bay Packers.